NO TURNING
BACK

For B-pa,
who taught me to be grateful
for everything and to live a life of
adventure and fun.

For my dad,
If you weren't my dad, I would still
choose you as my friend.

A special thanks to my parents,
my siblings, my husband, and my
grandma Pat, who all read this
book when it was merely a rough
draft, and encouraged me to finish
it.

In loving memory of Mónica, who was my dad's friend and lawyer through one of his darkest hours.

No Turning Back

Cover Designed by: Alethia Stendal & Stephen Miller
Layout and Illustrations by Stephen Miller
Layout Editing by Martha Jaramillo
Cover based on a painting by Raysa Abril
Editors: Michelle Burnham, Laurie Miller,
Pat Stendal
Published by Ransom Press International

Scripture quotations are taken from the Jubilee Bible, copyright 2020, by Ransom Press International. All Rights Reserved.

ISBN: Paperback: 978-1-64765-018-6
eBook: 978-1-64765-019-3

Printed in Colombia

Contents

    Let Us Return to the Roots of Our
    Godly Heritage
    A Sermon by Russell M. Stendal

NO TURNING BACK

by Alethia Stendal

Illustrations by Stephen Miller

"Deliver me not over unto the will of my enemies: for false witnesses are risen up against me and such as breathe out cruelty. I had fainted unless I had believed to see the goodness of the LORD in the land of the living. Wait for the LORD: be of good courage, and he shall strengthen thine heart; wait, I say, for the LORD."
Psalm 27:12-14

Introduction

February 19, 2015, 3:30 p.m. in a courtroom in Bogotá Colombia

"YOU HAVE two options: since you are an American citizen, the law allows you to return to your home. Should you choose that option, we would cancel this hearing, and you would be sent on a flight to the United States immediately. Never again would you be able to return to Colombia." The grave and unrelenting forty-something-year-old woman judge with curly black hair and prescription glasses looked sternly at my father.

"However, if you decide to stay," she continued, "and you face these charges and are declared guilty, you could be imprisoned for fifteen years and possibly more. It is your choice."

Minutes before, the prosecutor had made his opening statement projecting only hatred and contempt toward my father, a missionary charged with rebellion. The prosecution had arrogantly concluded that my dad was a menace to Colombia and should be forced to leave the country immediately, never to return again. If he *did* return, for the count of rebellion, he could face a minimum of fifteen years in a maximum-security prison.

What if my dad chose to stay and was declared guilty by this judge? Everything that had led up to this moment gave us absolutely no reason to believe there would be justice. The government had been underhandedly working on the case against him for more than two years. Only two months before, a recording had been given to us from an anonymous source saying there was a warrant out for Dad's arrest. No one had bothered to inform him of the situation, not even when he had sent someone to the district attorney's office to investigate. However, Dad had recently flown to a convention in Canada and had not been detained at the airport. Because of this, we assumed the case against him had been dropped. If there had been a warrant out for his arrest, surely the computers at the airport would have discovered it.

The prosecutor had been gathering "evidence" for years. Hundreds of pages of what he claimed were "testimonies" from false witnesses were now heaped on his desk. On the other hand, we'd had only one very short night to make up Dad's defense. On the defenses' desk lay a couple of Jubilee Bibles my dad had edited in English and Spanish, as well as a handful of other books he had written throughout the years. The police had arrested him the night before by covertly setting a trap. The press had already shamed and ridiculed him nationally and internationally, proclaiming his guilt on headline news before the hearing had even begun. The cold demeanor of the judge terrified us and the odds seemed to be undeniably stacked against my dad.

As I sat in the courtroom, the paradox of the situation flooded into my mind. The world was upside down and injustice was being dealt to a just man. A man who would break his back, trudge through sleet, hail or mud just to bring food to a family of farmers in need. Sometimes I would go with him.

I watched him drive, hike or ride mules through the most rugged and dangerous terrains only to help an outcast no one else gave a penny for. Very often the trails we would ride the mules on were very wet and slippery. On these winding mountain paths, if the mule missed a step, it could send you tumbling down hundreds of feet below. I was never really hurt on my jungle trips with Dad but he had been wounded on numerous occasions. Every once in a while, the mules did miss their steps and Dad would roll down with them. Miraculously the misstep never completely sent him off the edge, (if it had, he would've died,) but it did give him a few broken bones, more than once. One time he broke his wrist. Another time he broke a few ribs, and another time he hurt his neck badly. Sometimes we would walk through fields that were mined. In these sorts of places, my father would tell me to only step where he stepped. He knew what the mines looked like and I didn't.

It didn't matter if it was dangerous, if the gas and tollbooths cost him all his savings, or

if he hadn't slept the night before. Nothing ever stopped him. Not even broken bones. He would set up radio stations in places that were so God forsaken, no Colombian civilians would dare set foot, much less Americans. These radio stations became beacons of light to the forgotten hostages being held deep in the jungles. Many of them who were later released attested to this.

His red truck became famous in these war-torn areas. Women, children, men, and soldiers would see or hear the rumble of the truck from afar and come running down the countryside to flag down the *gringo*. They knew the red truck was full of Bibles and books for them. But no book or film could ever begin to describe the immeasurable ways in which the Lord had used my dad for the good of this nation. Colombia was so blessed to have someone like him fighting for her.

Regardless of whether or not it was my father, a man like this should be venerated and respected. But like every true man of God in the history of humanity, he was facing the hate of the world.

I looked at the judge's stern, intimidating eyes and wondered what my father would decide. She had laid the choice before him. He could face the trial or leave Colombia forever. "Choose the States," I prayed, "Who knows what will happen to you here."

The courtroom was packed full of our closest friends and about thirty reporters – all who anxiously awaited his response.

"I choose to face the trial." His kind, honest blue eyes looked fiercely at the judge, "I am not guilty."

I could feel my heart racing. The fight was on and there was no turning back.

Above: One of my many trips with Dad.

A girl and her mom stop Dad's red truck
to receive a Bible. The bushes behind are the "road".
It was a good thing the truck
is four wheel drive.

Dad checking on one of the radio stations.

Chapter 1

Ketchikan

August 17, 2008, Ketchikan, Alaska: six and one-half years before dad's trial.

GRANDPA CHAD Stendal, called B-pa by all of his grandchildren, had a remarkable spirit of discovery and adventure that played an important role in enabling him to become a missionary to the Kogi Indigenous people of the Sierra Nevada Mountains of Colombia. This same spirit of adventure led him to venture to Alaska in a time when it was not common for a Minnesota-born person to do so. The first time he went to Alaska was in 1952, when he was the civil engineer in charge of building what would later be known as the Richardson Highway. When I was a child, he would take me up this road with my grandmother and the rest of my family.

We would begin in Minnesota and cross all of Canada and then go on to Alaska. Sometimes we would go up past the Arctic

Circle to the land of the Eskimos. B-pa related
with the Eskimos because he came from a
similar background himself: the Vikings of
Norway.

The wonderful thing about traveling with
B-pa was that if he ever saw a mountain he
liked along the highway, he would simply
pull over and hike it. Dad inherited this
extraordinary quality of discovery from B-pa.
(I saw dad do this often as well, but in the
dangerous mountains of Colombia to put
up radio transmitters.) Being a fisherman at
heart, if there was a lake he thought might be
good for it, my grandpa would stop the motor
home and cast his pole in. The motor home
fit all kinds of stuff in it, including a portable
canoe on the top. With a twinkle in his eye,
B-pa always said, "The secret to being a good
fisherman is that you have to be smarter than
the fish." And did he ever catch the biggest
fish! They were his personal trophies. But I
was too little to fully enjoy the North and all
the adventures it brought back then.

That is, until one day when I was twenty-
one years old, and my dad asked me to help

B-pa and Grandma drive up the Richardson Highway. Although they were still active, they were getting older and the bulk of the trip would be too hard on them. I hadn't been up that road since I was thirteen years old. At first, I did not want to go because I thought I had too much work. My sister, Lisa, and I were busy making documentaries and writing our very first full-feature movie script.

But my dad told me all of that could wait and that I should reconsider. It ended up being a life-altering decision, and I am eternally thankful I made the right choice. For the first time in my life, I felt as though I was truly able to discover the magic found in driving up to Alaska, even though I had lost track of the number of times we had driven up there as a child. It is like everything in life. Sometimes you read a book and it just doesn't click for you, then ten years later the Lord ignites a light in your heart, and when you read it again, it comes to life in a way you had never imagined it would, and you are never the same.

B-pa was too old to enjoy himself like he had before, but he made sure I did. He knew every mountain that was good to hike up, every hot spring worth wading in, and every lake with big fish worth catching. I would be driving, and he would say, "Pull over right here. I want you and Misty to hike up this trail."

My cousin Misty and I would do as he said and trudge up the mountain, while Grandma and B-pa waited for us in the van. In our three-month road trip we saw bears, moose, wolves, foxes, ducks, caribou, mountain goats, northern lights dancing in magnificent colors, (the stars shining so big we thought we had never seen stars before,) and beautiful white pine trees so enormous, that it would take two or three people to hug them. I even got to catch and smoke my very own trout for the first time in my life, and it was mouth-watering to say the least.

Richard Wurmbrand's words couldn't be truer when he wrote, "There is no atheism among those brought up in nature." According to him, atheists were found where all of God's creation was covered with concrete.[1]

We drove all the way up to Anchorage and then on down to Haines, where we took a ferry to Juneau and then another ferry to Hoonah, Alaska. Hoonah was the destination my grandpa had been looking forward to the most. All along the Richardson Highway, B-pa would keep reminding me that we still had the ferries to look forward to and the beautiful Sitka spruce trees from Hoonah. To get there we sailed on ferries where the American flag stood tall, waving in the wind, and we could see the wonderful, pure northern ocean for miles around with the glorious snow-capped mountains beyond. And then once we were done with the big ferries, we took a small five-person boat to an island beyond the island of Hoonah where we would meet the loveliest people and see the most beautiful horses.

It was there that dazzling and enchanting, wild but tame, Norwegian horses nuzzled our

---

1   Richard Wurmbrand, Reaching Toward the Heights, page 57.

hands to get us to give them those deliciously tart and sweet Alaskan blueberries they knew we had just picked. Somehow they knew where to find us, and unlike most horses I had ever seen, they were fearless. Not even strangers from a distant land could intimidate them. It wasn't hard to see why the North is known as God's country. In this land, the women wore black rubber boots and guns tucked around their waist, as they did their farm chores without fear of the bears. But beyond their attire, they always carried a kind, warm smile. They were tough and nice at the same time. "Cool!" I thought.

I wrote a little something in my journal regarding the land of the midnight sun that now comes to mind:

The days are long
The nights are clear
I hear his voice that draws me near
I see a face that brings me cheer
I once forgot
I once was lost
But now I know He loves me, a lot
He draws me closer to his heart

When He is here, I have no fear
My help in times of trouble
A Savior, A King, and my Father
He has won in my life
He has set me free
And with him, I will spend eternity
Awake my soul and sing!
To the One who died for me!
The sun will rise when we sing
To Him who brought us into life
And has rid us from all strife

From there we hopscotched on a few more ferries until we finally found our way to Ketchikan, Alaska, a historic city for my family and me because it was there that my dad finished writing his first book called *Rescue the Captors.*[2] This book is the story he wrote about his first kidnapping by a Marxist guerrilla group, back in 1983. Many people in Alaska and Canada had read the book and wanted to meet him

2   Russell Stendal, Rescue the Captors: True Hostage Situation Involving Colombian Marxist Guerrillas and a Missionary (Ransom Press International)

personally. This paved the way for us to make friends up in the North and gave us a reason to continually return.

In Ketchikan my grandparents spoke at a church on Sunday, August 17, 2008. Sitting next to me was a man about five or six years older than me who was kneeling and lifting his hands in the air as he worshiped God fervently. I have to admit that I judged him a little. I had never seen someone be so overly passionate at a church service. "Tone it down a notch or two," I thought. But I pretended not to notice and continued singing.

I left as soon as the meeting ended, but later discovered that after the service, this man found Misty and told her he had an important message to give me. (She had also been standing with me at the service.)

The next day, as I was trying to rest a little before supper, Misty walked into my room; she told me that the man who was kneeling next to us was here to talk to me. I thought, "Oh no, it's that weirdo from the meeting." The last thing I wanted to do was talk to a weirdo.

Nevertheless, I got ready for the dinner our hostess had made — a most delicious salmon meal (afterward I decided it was perhaps the best salmon I had ever had). We all sat down to eat, and this man from the service and his wife began to tell us the story of how they met and fell in love and then got married. She was Alaskan and he was from Puerto Rico. Although I can't remember all the details, my opinion regarding him completely changed. I remember thinking, "Wow, he really loves her, and she is such a sweet and humble girl."

I thought it was so special how the Lord had worked it out miraculously so that they could be together. Their whole story seemed to be especially for me, even though there were about five other people also listening to it. After we ate dinner, the man suggested we move into the living room to continue talking. My grandma, Misty, and I sat down with the couple to continue the conversation. This time he became serious and said, "Alethia, God has brought me here to tell you one thing and one thing only."

"Okay…" I answered a bit taken aback, "What is it?"

"God has given you a crown, and you need to cherish it. Do not give it to the wrong man. The right man will respect you."

When he said this, I knew it was the truth. But I also knew that because it was the truth, it would be hard. When the Lord speaks clearly like that, it is not because it is going to be easy. He gives you that clear word because it is going to be really hard, and sometimes that reminder is the only little light you will be able to see. It is sort of like what happened to Jill Pole, the character in the book called *The Silver Chair*, when Aslan gave her the signs needed in order to find the lost prince. Although it was wonderful that Aslan was speaking to her and giving her signs, what lay ahead was going to be dark and require every bit of courage and strength she had to get through it.[3]

---

3   The Silver Chair by C. S. Lewis, published by Geoffrey Bles in 1953, was the fourth published of seven novels in The Chronicles of Narnia (1950–1956)

It was those few words of Aslan, the great Lion (a representation of God himself), that would keep her on target in the darkest times. Somehow, in a moment, I knew this would also be the case with me. I was happy that God had spoken to me but also apprehensive of what lay ahead.

Then the man prayed for me. After he finished, I said thank you from the bottom of my heart and I never saw them again.

On our way beyond Hoonah

Norwegian horses

Grandma and me at mile zero of the Alaskan Highway.

Chapter 2
Grandpa Plays the Piano

I HAD ALWAYS heard that B-pa was a concert pianist back in the day but that he had given up on that dream to serve in World War II. When he came back, he studied to become a civil engineer and headed up many projects in Minnesota. He soon felt a calling of God on his life to something different, and after studying linguistics, he and his whole family went to Colombia to be missionaries. His career in piano playing became a distant memory. No one in our family had ever heard him play.

Misty, who had to get back to Florida since she was still in high school, flew home again from Vancouver, leaving me on this trip with just my grandparents. We had been on the road for more than two months, driving all the way up to Alaska and were now on our way back to Minnesota. During this time, B-pa had never once driven the car. He used a cane to walk, and most of the time, he just

sat, whether he was in a car or in a house.
A hip replacement surgery years before had
gotten the better of him, and he had more
or less given up on himself. Dad and others
would talk about who B-pa used to be before,
but none of us from my time had ever seen
the true Chadwick Martín Stendal. We only
saw our old, worn out grandfather sitting in a
chair. Grandma was now in charge of running
everything.

As special guests in a church in Vancouver,
the pastor asked B-pa to speak about the
missionary work in Colombia. B-pa limped up
to the microphone with his cane, and as soon
as he tried to speak, he started to weep. I had
never seen him cry before. After a minute, he
composed himself enough to say in a weak,
almost inaudible voice, "I am only a man in
desperate need of prayer."

Everyone stayed frozen, as if no one in the
church was expecting this. Since no one else
seemed to know what to do, I got up and
prayed for him. I asked the Lord to make
him walk again as he had walked before. I
probably prayed other things that I don't

remember now, and our good friend Jean Bergeron stood up with me and she also prayed for him.

After the meeting ended and the people had left, my grandpa came and sat next to me.

"How would you like to accompany me to a Gershwin concert tonight?" he asked.

"Umm, I don't know B-pa. I was actually thinking of going to the movies. I don't really know who Gershwin is." It didn't sound very interesting to me.

His face dropped to a saddened frown, "You don't know who Gershwin is?"

"No, not really." I responded honestly.

Without hesitation, he got right out of his chair and walked to the other end of the room where an old piano stood. He sat down and positioned his hands on the piano with his back straight like a true pianist would and played me the most beautiful composition I had ever heard anyone play. Grandma stood behind me, mouth open, completely astounded. I heard her say, "My land! I have

not heard him play like that in over thirty years! I didn't know he still had it in him."

After he finished, he walked back to me and said, "That is a composition by Gershwin that I played for you. Now would you like to come with me tonight?"

I could not believe it.

"Of course I'll come with you B-pa! I would love to!" I exclaimed.

The concert was magical. I have been to many concerts, but that one was by far the best one I had ever been to before and since then. The performers made me believe and breathe what they were singing and what they were playing like no other musicians had ever done for me. They sang songs from *Oklahoma*, the musical, and from *The Wizard of Oz*. But the one they were honoring that night was George Gershwin. So the pianist played *Rhapsody in Blue* among other compositions.

My grandpa whispered to me, "He is a wonderful pianist! I am going to be sure to congratulate him when this is over."

The concert ended, and B-pa went to the restroom. When he came back, he had the biggest smile on his face. "I met the pianist as I was washing my hands. I was about to congratulate him, but he turned to me first and congratulated me! He said he had read all my books and really admired everything the Lord had done through me in Colombia."

"That is really special B-pa." I smiled.

Fun times with Grandma and Grandpa.

Chapter 3

The Drive Home

WE STILL had a long way to go on our
return trip before getting all the way
back to Grand Rapids, Minnesota, to my
grandparent's lake cabin.

At some point along the way, I encouraged
my grandfather to drive again. He hadn't
driven in years, and my grandma was a little
nervous about it. But just like he hadn't
forgotten how to play the piano, he hadn't
forgotten how to drive either. Soon he was the
one who was behind the wheel most of the
time.

B-pa made sure we drove the scenic
route so that I could see everything and
take pictures. We saw the Canadian Rocky
Mountains and the Yellowstone National
Park. It was one of the most beautiful drives
I had ever been on. And when I didn't think
the view could get any better, a double
rainbow appeared. I sat in the passenger seat
excitedly snapping pictures of lovely green

and yellow hills and the two full-sized colorful rainbows against the clear blue sky. When I turned to look down at my camera, I saw that the pictures didn't have the same vibrant color they did while I was snapping them. I wondered what had happened! Then I realized that the whole time I was taking pictures, I had rose-tinted sunglasses on, and they had made things seem a lot more breathtaking to me than they really were!

B-pa and Grandma laughed when I told them what had happened. I took my sunglasses off, and as we drove on, the scenery kept on getting more beautiful by the minute. The sunset began to make everything more colorful and alive. Little gophers along the hilly lands came out to look at our car as we drove by, and the sun lit them perfectly. And then the sunset came, and I saw the round, orange sun suddenly sink into the horizon in a split second. Orange and pink lit up one part of the heavens, and the sliver of a new moon with a bright star next to it appeared on the other side.

Then B-pa said with his raspy, sweet voice that always characterized him, "You know Alethia, I think the Lord is trying to show you something. I think he wants you to know that what he has for you is more beautiful than anything you could see through rosy-colored glasses."

The next day, I encouraged him to try walking without a cane. "You can do it B-pa. I know you can."

"You think so?" He smiled.

"I know so."

He began to practice walking without a cane. I could see this newfound confidence in himself was making him happier. We went to a church that wanted to honor him and Grandma. They told us they wanted Grandma and Grandpa to dress in white, in honor of the typical white garments the Kogis wear. B-pa and Grandma were to walk through the entire church as a bride would when she is meeting her groom with everyone standing and clapping for them. They wanted to honor the missionaries they had supported for so many years. A boy in the church led them, carrying a pole with a huge yellow, blue, and red Colombian flag on it. My grandparents followed close behind, smiling and happier than I had ever seen them.

Grandpa was glad to have practiced walking without a cane because when that day came, he was able to walk the whole way alone and without a limp while hundreds of people watched and applauded him and Grandma.

* * *

It was night and we were really close to getting to our lovely lake cabin in the woods when green northern lights appeared in the sky. B-pa stopped the car, and I jumped out to look at them. They were a distance away from us, but I could still see them clearly. B-pa got out of the car as well, something he would have never done before. When we first got there, they were unmoving, yet fascinating.

"I heard that if you whistle, they will dance," my grandpa said. Even though it was dark out and we were both facing the lights,

I could imagine the twinkle in his eyes as he spoke. Slowly, at the sound of B-pa's gentle whistle, the northern lights began to sway back and forth showing their colors in more beauty and splendor than ever before. It was one of those rare and beautiful moments that I will cherish forever – the night when Grandpa and me whistled and the northern lights danced.

Some people love mountains. Some love the ocean. Others prefer the desert. Although I enjoy all of these landscapes, going to the land of the 10,000 lakes (Minnesota) has made me realize that I love nothing more than the magic of those delicate maple trees and their beautiful fresh green leaves, the grandeur of the pine trees, and the crystal clear, blue, deliciously fresh lakes that they surround. It is delightful to swim in them because they are as blue as the Caribbean Sea, but instead of being salty, they are as sweet and pure to the taste and to the skin as the cleanest river. You can also wade and relax in them without having to counteract the strong pull of the ocean waves or the heavy current of a river.

Minnesota is wonderful. Somehow, when I'm there my energy level triples. It's a little slice of heaven on earth.

I could feel the magic in the night air as the wind rustled through the trees and we approached the little cabin in the woods. (Grandpa had designed his very own lake cabin, when good friends from his past gave him the land and helped him build his special dream.)

B-pa made the moment of arrival even more special by singing. We had been through a long road trip. The Lord had helped us through many things. It was a song fit for the occasion.

"My God is good to me; my God is good to me." His sweet voice sang, "He holds my hand. He helps me stand. He's good to me." In his case, the words, "he helps me stand," were literal.

I went home again to Colombia with a fire ignited in me and a new promise.

* * *

Later that year, a letter arrived in the mail for me. It was from my grandpa.

Sept 28, 2008

Dear Alethia,

It is so beautiful here at the cabin as the leaves are changing to so many wonderful colors. I am so sorry you are not here to see it. A fat grey and a black squirrel are running around hiding acorns in the ground for next winter, and a great American eagle with his white head and tail is flying back and forth. Four deer are in our woods and are almost tame.

I praise the Lord daily for your friendship. It is the nicest thing the Lord has ever done for me. I praise him for making a woman so delightful and beautiful both spiritually and physically.

I am getting better and have help from a chiropractor and physical therapy. Most of all, your faith that I will recover inspires me.

I trust your birthday went well.
I can hardly wait to see you again. I
should be arriving in Colombia on the
second of November.
Love, Chad

A short time later, a guy from the States
began writing me letters. I had known him
from before, and because I had nice memories
of him, I wrote him back. Seven months later,
this guy came to Colombia. Whatever rose-
colored glasses I had when he was writing me
were immediately removed the day he arrived,
and I remembered that warning again: "You
have been given a crown. Cherish it. Do not
give it to the wrong man…the right man will
respect you."

The Lord would not have mentioned a
"wrong man" if there wasn't going to be one.
I could tell this guy did not respect me, even
though back then I did not know what the
whole meaning of the word respect meant.
Words are powerful and have such immense
meaning that sometimes they are more than
what our minds can comprehend, and we only

scratch the surface of what they were meant
to portray. Years later, another boy would
come who would show me exactly what the
word meant. But in this moment I had to deal
with only vaguely knowing the meaning of
it. Because of God's promise to me, I knew to
call it off immediately.

It was not an easy thing to go through,
but the Lord was so good to speak to me
about it beforehand. He knew it would be
hard, and he knew I would need that assur-
ance from him to hold on to. Jill Pole – in the
dark underworld with only the words spoken
from Aslan to give her hope and guide her –
couldn't have been a better picture as to how I
felt. At the end of the story, Jill passes the test
and finds the lost prince, not because she was
so good but instead because the Lord was so
good to her.[4]

* * *

One day, we were having a family dinner
and I was feeling a little sad inside, although

4   From C.S. Lewis, The Silver Chair.

I thought I was doing a good job at hiding it. My compassionate, beautiful, and kind-hearted little three-year-old niece, Gabriella, read right through me as if I were an open book.

"Auntie, don't worry," she spoke sternly. Then she looked at me full of the empathy and sweetness that only a child can give and said, "You are a princess, and one day, you will marry a prince."

My beautiful niece and BFF, Gabriella Eden.

Fishing with B~pa

I love to eat fish, I don't like to hold them.

Chapter 4
Noah

THROUGHOUT the next year, my sister Lisa and I had a blast working on many projects, including the recording of the Jubilee Bible in English for the radio. During this time, Lisa was pregnant with her second child, Isaac Judah. She read the Scriptures in her beautiful, soothing radio voice, while I listened intently for any mistakes and our friend Fernando Alarcon recorded it. Truly wonderful things have come from the small recording studio we dug out of the mountainside of my parent's apartment in the city.

When my dad began to send us to a small Missionary school in Bogotá, we were required to bring our own Bible. My dad began looking at all the different versions to see which was the best one to give his daughters.

During that time, someone gave him a copy of Casiodoro de Reina's original Bible from the 1500's. Casiodoro was one of the

last translators of the Bible to have known
Hebrew while it was still a living language.
Hebrew would not resurrect again for another
500 years.

Dad began comparing all the modern
translations to this old Spanish edition and
found that none lived up to it. So in an effort
to give his children the best translation
possible, he began working on his own
edition. One that would be based off of the
work of William Tyndale and Casiodoro de
Reina.

For ten years of my childhood, I saw him
working fervently on this endeavor. He would
do his missionary work, speak at meetings,
tour up in the North, but at night, when
no one else was awake, he would work until
four or five in the morning. Like the god-
daughter that inspired C.S. Lewis to write
what would be his greatest life achievement:
the Chronicles of Narnia, my sister and I also
inspired what we consider is our dad's greatest
life achievement: the Jubilee Bible.

It was the first time I had ever heard the
Bible from beginning to end when Lisa read

it for the radio. There is something truly amazing that happens when someone else reads you a book. It is as if something that had only been two dimensional came into the third dimension.

Only the Lord could have inspired people like William Tyndale, Casiodoro de Reina and my dad, to make sure this manuscript was kept alive. For the first time, I knew why it was possible for men like Casiodoro de Reina and William Tyndale to be willing to be burnt at the stake for their life work. I saw what they had seen: the life, the love and the power behind every single word.

Dad always said that back then the enemy's tactic was to burn everyone, along with their Bibles. But now the strategy has changed. Instead, the enemy uses something a little more tricky: watered down versions that have lost the fire and the true meaning of what the Lord really meant.

During this time, Lisa and I discovered that every single author in the Bible has so much personality and character. For example, Luke was a natural storyteller. It was funny to see

how Mark loved repeating the fact that Judas was the one who had betrayed Jesus. Just in case we had forgotten.

We found that John was one of those special people. Some were present for the miracles, others appeared after the resurrection. Almost everyone was too afraid and either hid or watched him die from afar. But John was there during the Lord's darkest hour and was even entrusted with the Lord's mother. John was "that disciple whom Jesus loved". No other great accomplishments did he write for himself. That was good enough for him.

We discovered that Paul's court case in the book of Acts would make the greatest movie of all times. Strangely, every single time we would try to record the book of Acts, something would happen. There would either be too much noise outside or sometimes the computer would simply shut down. After many failed attempts at recording this particular book, I began to wonder why. Some people may think this sounds strange but if a book wasn't so important, hundred's of people wouldn't have died throughout the centuries just to preserve it. The text survived, but it came with the price of many.

Then it suddenly clicked and I realized that the enemy is okay with the fact that Jesus was here thousands of years ago, doing miracles. He can tolerate stories from before, like that of Moses, of Joshua, of Noah. But the book of Acts in particular talks about the Resurrection of the Lord Jesus Christ happening! In other words, it was no longer a prophesy. That was what Paul's trial was all about making it so fascinating to read. Paul got into so much trouble just for saying that the Lord had resurrected! When I noticed this, I began by praying before every single recording session until we finally got through this book. Not many people want a resurrected Jesus, and especially not the enemy. A baby in a manger is okay. A man on a cross is fine. But the resurrected Lord means that death has been defeated and the enemy has lost his power.

What I loved the most about the Scriptures was discovering that every single book in

the Old Testament was prophesying the resurrection.

Job says in Chapter 19: 23-27, *"Oh, that my words were now written! Oh, that they were printed in a book! That they were graven with an iron pen and lead in the rock for ever! For I know that my redeemer lives and that he shall rise at the latter day over the dust; and afterward from this, my stricken skin and from my own flesh, I must see God: whom I shall see for myself, and my eyes shall behold, and not another, though my kidneys be consumed within me."*

Job knew his redeemer was going to resurrect from the dust and that even though his body would be consumed within him (in other words death), he would be transformed to see his Lord.

Job 14:13,14 *"O that thou would hide me in Sheol, that thou would keep me covered until thy wrath is past, that thou would appoint me a set time and remember me! If a man dies, shall he live again? All the days of my appointed time I will wait until my transformation comes."*

In Job's time, the Lord had not yet died and resurrected, defeating death forever. But Job would wait for that day, even if he had to wait in Sheol. He knew that the Lord would bring him out of the dust at the appointed time. He was prophesying the resurrection.

I found that Job was the best poet, even though maybe Solomon and David get more recognition in this respect.

We thought that the Song of Solomon must have been a play performed for all the nobility of that day. Lisa made a different voice for each character.

The personality of each writer shone through in a way in which I had never before experienced. But more than that, all the people who wrote the Scriptures had one thing in common: they were all moved by the love and fear of the Almighty God, so much that they were willing to go through fire and even death for every single written word. The translators and transcribers who came after, were also willing to do this, and that is why the text remains to this day.

I came to love the Word of God being read to me, and sometimes I would have my dad read me a couple of chapters from the book of Psalms.

However, on the morning of my twenty-third birthday, my beautiful Colombian mom read to me instead. She chose Psalm 23. After she finished, she gave me a necklace with the word "Noah" engraved on it and said, "I am certain that one day you will marry a wonderful man and have a son named Noah." She knew that Noah was my favorite name and my favorite Bible story and that I had always dreamed of naming my son after him.

Dad showing us secrets from the old manuscripts of the Bible.

Chapter 5
The "Old Man" From Florida

More than five years after Ketchikan, Alaska

DURING THESE five years we filmed a movie script we had written called La Montaña as well as other shorter films about our work in Colombia. I had many adventures with my dad in the jungles and mountains of the country and took tons of pictures and footage of everything I saw. Many times I was invited to speak abroad about my experiences. And although I was having the time of my life working on things that I absolutely loved, there was still a void inside.

Making a movie had been my lifelong dream, but deep down I knew that what I really wanted the most was to have a family. I wanted to be part of those few and privileged individuals who get to know what it is like to love and to be loved. This was my true desire. The prophecies and the prayers concerning this became a distant memory held deep in

the back of my mind, almost forgotten. That was about to change.

* * *

October 31, 2013, Bogotá, Colombia

A few months earlier, in June, my sister Lisa received a message from an old high school friend. Lisa met Stephanie when she went up to Alaska to graduate from high school at the age of fourteen. (As a result of all the trips up north when we were little and all the friends my parents had made, she had decided that Alaska was the place where she wanted to graduate.) Stephanie had a little brother who wanted to learn Spanish and needed a place to stay in Colombia. He wanted to be in a remote town in the middle of nowhere, where no one spoke English, and Stephanie asked Lisa to help him out. Matchmaker Lisa and my brothers looked him up on Facebook and saw that he was cute *and* he was my age. Perfect! They thought.

My very astute sister and well-meaning mom were setting me up! They all knew he was coming, but no one told me anything.

When the day of his arrival came, Lisa made sure that all the guys – the ones who usually picked people up from the airport – were gone for the day. Then she left too, and called me up saying, "Oh, I forgot to tell you. This old man is coming in today from Florida and no one else is home. Can you pick him up?"

"Who is he?" I asked.

"I don't know, some old man from Florida that wants to look at the radio stations or something like that. I really don't know much about him. I guess he's one of dad's old friends," she slyly stated.

"Well, can you send me a picture, 'cause how am I supposed to know who he is?"

"I don't have a picture, okay? Just write down his name on a piece of paper and wave it at the people that come off the plane. His name is Stephen Miller."

Naively, I wrote the name Stephen Miller on a blank piece of paper with a really light-colored purple pen I found. It was the only pen around.

I only had half an hour to get to the airport. When I got there, I ran in, thinking I was already late, and frantically started to

wave the piece of paper to all the old men that walked by. After many attempts, I thought that maybe the old men were not able to see the writing, since it was written with the light purple ink, so I began to wave the paper really close to every old man that came out the door, just to make sure this Stephen Miller wouldn't miss it.

Pretty soon everyone else who came to pick people up started smiling at me. After about thirty minutes this tall, dark-haired, handsome guy started waving in my direction. I looked behind me to see who he was waving at, but there was no one there. Since he could see I was not getting the message, he walked to where I was, bent low and looked into my face, and with a big smile on his face, waved at me again.

At last I realized that this was Stephen Miller, and he was not from Florida; he was from Alaska. And did he ever look Alaskan! It was as if he had just returned from hunting a moose.

I drove him home, and when I parked the big pick-up truck in the small Bogotá parking lot, he said that if I were in Alaska, he would hire me immediately to work in his dad's construction company since I handled the truck so well. Next he offered me watermelon candy. My favorite. Two points for him there, and we had only known each other for an hour.

That night we had a karaoke party at my house with all my friends, and Stephen made us all homemade pretzels; –Third point! –

Stephen liked the fact that my karaoke party not only included my friends but my friends' parents as well, and my brothers, sister, and my little niece and nephew. He fit into our family like he had always known us. There was never an awkward moment, and my mom – who usually gets tired of newcomers quickly – didn't get tired of him.

Before then, my closest friends knew me best as a creep magnet. I really don't know what it was about me, but the creepiest guys would literally stalk me. They would come so far as to say, "The Lord told me to marry you."

To that I would reply, "That's great, but the Lord hasn't told me anything!"

Some would have dreams and visions about me being their wife, or sometimes their mom would have the dream, and they would write

me about it. One even asked my dad for my hand in marriage when I wasn't even friends with the guy! These American and Canadian guys all had one thing in common: they all said God had told them they needed to "help out" in the mission here in Colombia. As soon as I would turn them down, whatever "word from the Lord" they had received about helping would suddenly vanish and we wouldn't hear back from them.

Stephen came to Colombia with a clear intention: to learn Spanish. He didn't know anything about any "mission" or my family, nor did he care to know about it. He wasn't saying anything about the Lord, or about what he had heard the Lord say to him. He was just a very pleasant guy to be around.

As he was making the pretzels, my mom looked at me and said in Spanish, "You know, back when I met your dad, he was a skinny little thing just like this guy is, and no one gave a nickel for him. Don't write this guy off. He's going to be something one day."

Chapter 6
Abuelita's Approval

"WOULD YOU like to go to La Vega with me tomorrow?" I asked this cute new guy from Alaska.

He decided to come, even though he was supposed to study Spanish at the town of Garzón, Huila, where a family was waiting for him. The very next day after he got here, we were going down a winding road, with a beautiful backdrop of the Colombian Andes Mountains in my two-person truck.

My cute, funny, friendly, and just-plain-adorable indigenous maternal grandma, Abuelita Cecilia, was waiting for us at the farm owned by my aunt Rosario, uncle Segundo, and their daughter, Raysa, who is a year younger than me. Their beautiful bamboo home stands right in the middle of the stunning Andes Mountains, and my grandma has taught all her daughters the Yuruti Indigenous secrets of cooking. From the southeastern side of Colombia: it is – to

say the least – some of the best food ever.
There are no sauces, no spices. It is just fish
and salt, or beef and salt, but it is cooked in
plantain leaves for hours with only the smoke
of the coal and the wood, and it is simply
delicious. No five-star meal can compare to
the flavor that is found in this cooking.

To go with it, there are plantains, avocados,
rice, and always *casabe*, a bread made from
cassava, a wild form of Yuca that is poisonous
if you do not know how to process it. My
grandma makes amazing *casabe* that is grilled
and then magically enhanced with a little
butter and salt. In my opinion, this is better
than any bread. As we feasted, Stephen, who
is a foodie and a natural chef, fell in love
with the food and my family (especially my
grandmother).

The next morning, Segundo and my cousin
Raysa went out to pick coffee beans from the
farm, and my grandmother taught Stephen
how to grind the freshly roasted beans for our
morning coffee. As he spun the grinder over
and over again, my grandma looked at me and
then pointed at him and gave me a thumbs up
sign right as he turned to look at us. I was so

embarrassed. My grandma had just given me her approval for him, and he had seen it. Then she looked at him, grabbed his hair and said in her thick Indigenous accent in Spanish, "You are a nice boy, but nice boys don't have long hair! You need get it cut!"

Stephen and Abuelita

Chapter 7

Ernesto's Prophecy

MY NINE-MONTH sickness saga began in the northern coast of the country where I got food poisoning. This led to months where I did not feel well and had constant stomach problems. Then I went to Disney World, and unbeknown to me, my appendix ruptured on one of the rides. What I thought were period cramps ended up being a major infection of my insides that would have killed me had I not been operated on in time. The full recovery of my body took six months and had left me very weak. I was just beginning to feel good again.

To make a long story short, when Stephen got here, I was done being sick and ready for as many adventures as possible. After our visit to my grandmother's, we went back to Bogotá, where I planned my next trip. I was ready to take a break from the work in the city and travel the country. Garzón, Huila, was my next stop, and it was coincidentally the same town where Stephen wanted to study Spanish. My sister suggested I take advantage of this and drive him there. Little did I know of my mom and sister's conspiracy to get us together.

"Yes, Alethia, go to Huila with your girlfriends," my mom said. "You can take my car so that they all fit. Oh, and you might as well take Stephen too, since he is already going out there."

"Yeah, take Stephen too!" Lisa chimed in.

The striking generosity should have made me wonder, but it didn't.

Off we went to Huila in my mom's car with my good friend and cousin Raysa, my high school buddy Daniela, and Stephen. The seven-hour drive is breathtaking. I absolutely love it. The friends at the end of the road are even better. Ernesto and his wife, Nenfis, are the epitome of Colombian hospitality. The only person they knew in the whole crew was me, yet they had no problem when I called them and said I was arriving with five other friends. Johnny Porter, another Alaskan guy that came to visit, and our co-worker Abel

Parra were also on their way, and they were
bringing my dog Lucy.

Ernesto and Nenfis said yes without
batting an eye, and they proved – just
as everyone else I have visited in this
country has – that there is nothing like
Colombian hospitality. Their son Isaac took
us everywhere. We went to all of the rivers,
and Nenfis made *sancocho*, a Colombian
chicken stew, that warmed us right up after
swimming. Isaac took us to all the hot
springs, the caves, the waterfalls, the hidden
roads, the desert, the picturesque little towns,
and the ancient ruins left from Indigenous
tribes hundreds of years before. We were
having the time of our lives.

Stephen looked like Tarzan climbing up
the rocky walls in the midst of the waterfalls
and jumping off of them and into the water.
On one of our many stops, Isaac took us to
a restaurant called Tarzan. The whole place
was made out of wood, and it looked like a
huge treehouse in the middle of the jungle.
There was this big vine that you could swing
through the restaurant on. Stephen decided to

teach me how to swing. Down I went through the restaurant. Soon we had acquired new nicknames: Tarzan and Jane.

* * *

After two weeks, our visit came to an end, and Raysa and I did not know if we wanted to go back to Bogotá. I told Raysa that maybe our trip wasn't over, and we were supposed to go somewhere else before heading back to Bogotá. She said she felt the same way. We both prayed and felt that Cauca was the place we needed to go to next. Isaac said that we could go in his car since he wanted to go too. We could send my mom's car down the line back to Bogotá with Daniela.

We decided this was the best option and began packing. Stephen was supposed to have stayed behind "learning Spanish," but I invited him to come along with us to see that other side of the country. I don't know why, but I thought it was important that he come with us. He, on the other hand, felt he was getting side-tracked from his initial plan of learning Spanish. But I could feel that he wanted to come. Before leaving Alaska, his

dad had told him to let go and not be afraid of anything that might come up that was not according to his plans.

A few minutes before we left, Stephen ran down from his room with his backpack all ready to leave with us. God knows what would have happened had he stayed in that town, but I can tell you what happened because he left with us.

As we were saying our goodbyes to everyone, Ernesto came out of his room and said, "Alethia, I have a prophecy for you!"

I looked at him in surprise, "What is it?"

He answered, "You will be married this year..."

I thought he must be right because I had felt that way too.

Then he finished, "...to Stephen!"

My heart sank, "Not on your life, false prophet." I thought. But I only smiled at Ernesto and shoved it off as a joke.

Before leaving, Ernesto gathered us around his table to say a prayer. He always says that when people ask him to pray for them, he never likes to because unprecedented things happen afterward. He could write a book of all the stories he has lived through because of this. People ask for God to intervene in their lives or for God's justice to prevail, but seldom do they know what that really means.

God's justice is something to be afraid of if you are not clean. If priests in the Bible were unclean when going into God's presence, they would die. So with Ernesto; when friends of his would ask him for prayer on a certain situation, the Lord's response would frequently be a lot different than what they had hoped for. Hence, Ernesto does not like praying for people and says he hardly ever will.

On this occasion, it was Ernesto's decision to pray for us. We all sat down and closed our eyes. He prayed for our trip to Cauca and for Stephen. Strangely, as he was praying, I could feel a strong presence summoning Stephen, focusing on him, sort of beckoning him. After the prayer, Stephen went to the bathroom and Ernesto told me, "This prayer was for Stephen. I felt it."

"I felt it too," I said.

"You know Alethia, when I prayed for your trip, I saw Stephen's heart, a very black and dark heart, and the more time he passed traveling here, the whiter his heart turned, until eventually, it became pure white. His trip here to Colombia is no coincidence. God is going to do something. We just need to make sure we take all the right steps."

He looked at me as if I were taking the baton in a relay race. "This trip to Cauca is one of them."

Ernesto and his wife Nenfis
take Stephen for a boat ride.

Chapter 8
Pablo Escobar's House

WE DECIDED to drive through an unknown, unpaved road to Cauca. There was a route that was technically safer in the sense that there would be no guerrilla or paramilitary roadblocks, but it was also very dangerous as far as having to share a narrow, windy, uphill mountain road with huge semis that sometimes flipped over and could block the pass for hours. This narrow, windy road was also ten hours longer. Naturally, we decided to take the shortcut through the mountains on a not very famous road. Halfway along, Raysa and I exchanged a worried look. We didn't see any signs of the army.

Usually on Colombian roads it is normal to see soldiers patrolling the roads, keeping order, and giving big thumbs up signs to us to signal that the road is safe to travel on. Guerrillas have been noted for blowing up

bridges or taking hostages, which makes the government run a strong security program filling all the main roads with soldiers.

Raysa and I kept quiet, not wanting to scare everyone else, though deep inside I thought, "This is getting very lonely. There is no sign of the army. No other cars. What did we get ourselves into?"

Just when I was beginning to think it may have been a terrible idea to take the shortcut, we saw a big army base alongside the road, which made me feel a lot better. Raysa sighed in relief.

Later, Ernesto told us that only a few days after we had taken this unknown road, another car drove through it and did not make it through the other side. The two people traveling had been kidnapped, army base or no.

Thankfully, we made it unharmed to the other side of the mountain range to the city of Popayán and on to our house.

Stephen was silent when we got to the house, so I asked him what was the matter.

He said, "Nothing. I just wasn't expecting to walk into Pablo Escobar's house."[5]

The house we were in was right in the middle of the best golf course in the country and had a lake and a pool right in front of it with a large deck for the pool and a dock for the lake. For years, we had set up radio stations and passed out literature while staying in military bases. These bases were kept by soldiers, and though it was nice of the army to let us stay there, the work had gotten so intense that it became necessary to have a full-time base of our own.

Stephen was right, in a way, to look confused. Years back, mafiosos such as Pablo Escobar had built this golf course and many of their homes right on it. Then it had been taken over by the government, and they gave it to a doctor's association. Now, mostly doctors owned the club and the houses in it. The club even had a landing for a helicopter, a water park, a bowling alley, soccer fields,

---

5   Pablo Escobar was a Colombian drug lord and narcoterrorist who founded and was the sole leader of the Medellín Cartel.

and tennis courts. However, the increasing drug trade in the area, which the government seemed to turn a blind eye to (marijuana and cocaine labs and fields only thirty kilometers away from this bubble), had led to the area being filled with violence once again. This forced all the really rich people to leave and made the rent extremely low.

Hence, for the past six months our Finnish friends, who wanted to help us help the different Indigenous groups in Cauca, were renting this "Pablo Escobar" house for what it cost to rent out a small apartment in Bogotá, only because it was now considered a dangerous war zone. The club this house was located in also had something of vital importance for all the foreigners we brought down to help with the missionary work in Cauca: it provided a haven of security. We were living right next to a town known to have the most kidnappings in the country.

The United States has a Department of Security website that rates all the different countries on a scale from one to four, with one being the safest and four being the most dangerous. Though many parts of Colombia are in a number two category, Cauca falls into a number four category with bold letters next to it saying, DO NOT TRAVEL THERE.

On a dark night, one can see all the hills surrounding our house light up as if they were little towns. But upon careful observation you see that the color of the light is different; it has a hint of neon, and it is not one light here and there, as a little town would be lit up, but whole rectangles and squares that are illuminated at once. Dad says they are marijuana and cocaine fields that are lit up with special types of light bulbs in order to continue the growth without sunlight and therefore double the production.

Chapter 9

The Guambianos

DAD HAD over seven Christian radio stations he helped the different Indigenous communities run in the area by donating transmitters and any other radio equipment they needed. These Indigenous people do not need the usual required legal permission to have radio stations because they are in their own land reservations and basically abide by their own rules. As a result, if they want to do something good, no one can stop them, but if they want to end all our food production and replace it with coca and marijuana produce, supposedly the government can't stop them either. They also manage their own judicial system, and many of Christian faith have been severely persecuted in these areas for not following the traditional beliefs of their tribe.

Though Colombia as a whole, outside of these reservations, has freedom of religion, these Indigenous groups have lived through persecution from their very own people as bad

as the Christians did back in the dark ages.
Torture chambers, copied from the Spanish
Inquisition, are their method. Severe torture
scars are the norm for many of the Christians
there.

In spite of all this, the persecution had
lit a spark in these different groups and the
Colombian Army had noticed. Many generals
in the area told dad that his missionary
endeavor worked and that he had all their
support. Some of the people in these tribes
were known to throw police officers off of
hills, making them paralytics for the rest of
their lives. But when officers would make
presence with the Christian indigenous
groups, it was a completely different story.
They were now treated with respect.

A few months before, I had accompanied my
dad, who was invited to speak at a Guambiano
church near our home base in Cauca. I had
never been to a church of that sort before.
Several *chivas*, a typical colorful bus, drove in
packed full of smiling Guambianos who all
wore the same beautiful, colorful clothing.
The first part of the meeting was reserved for
testimonies from anyone who wanted to get

up and speak. Person after person got up to
say how Dad's radio stations had changed their
lives. For years these radio stations were on
the air, but we had only seen the studio side of
broadcasting – the programs and the messages
produced in our house. I had never seen the
effect of it all like I did that day.

The testimonies were all very similar. They
would say things like, "Now, after listening
to the radio stations, I know that we have to
overcome evil with good. We have to treat
even the soldiers and the policemen with
kindness." I smiled. It was a different story
when seen from their side.

* * *

Now, when I visited on Stephen's first trip
to Colombia, one of the main Indigenous
leaders who ran all those radio stations
was getting married, and he invited us as
honored guests to his wedding. Raysa, Isaac,
Stephen, and I all went to the wedding
in representation of my family. It was an
experience we will never forget. Never had
I seen such a colorful, simple, and beautiful
wedding.

A multitude of Guambianos surrounding
the church and the chiva.

Stephen meets the Guambianos.

Chapter 10

The Páez Community

WHILE IN CAUCA, we also went to see the Páez Nasa Indigenous community that my family had been helping for the past few years. The first time we met them was when our friend General Barrero lined it up for us to show our movie *La Montaña* to all the Christian Indigenous communities in the area.

On that earlier visit, we arrived with a huge theater screen and the latest audio equipment that played 5.1 theater sound, and hundreds of Páez's gathered around to watch it. We could hear them excitedly talking in their language and laughing at the funny parts.

It was sad, to say the least, to see how they were living. Years before, a natural disaster had destroyed their village and they had been displaced. The government had given the tribal leaders humanitarian aid and new land for their survival, but since these people were Christians, the tribal leaders excluded them from the humanitarian aid and even persecuted them for their faith. Many had terrible scars on their legs and on their arms because of the torture that they had to endure. They were forced to beg on the streets for a while, and then eventually they made a way to live in garbage houses. They had no toilets, no running water, just garbage bags with a few sticks over their heads and dirt floors.

Soon after the presentation of the movie, we went back to interview them. They told us their story and showed us their scars. It was evident that they needed a lot of help for just their basic necessities. However, when Dad asked their leader, Marco Tulio, what they needed the most, he moved us to tears with his response. "We need more Bibles." He said, "See we have Bibles, but our Indigenous neighbors do not. We would like to have the materials necessary to be able to witness to our enemies and show them the love of God."

It was their attitude that moved our hearts toward helping them. One of the main leaders in this endeavor has been my brother-in-law, Samuel Hernández, or Sammy, as we call him.

Sammy wrote a report describing the needs of these dear people, and pretty soon countries from all over the world wanted to help out.

A few weeks before we arrived in Cauca, Sammy and Lisa had just been there to help them move into their new God-given land. Here is the report written by my sister for the November 2013 newsletter:

Many times we work hours and hours for years and never get to see the full extent of the fruit of our labor. We just have to have faith that what we have invested so fervently in is worth it somewhere, to someone. But I would not say that this means that we go unrewarded in our labors of love, because every once in a while we get to reap the fruit of what others have sown. We get to witness firsthand the reward of another person's sweat and toil and be the great beneficiaries of the love others have invested. This happened to me this last week.

For months, Sammy and other people around the world have worked tirelessly and against amazing odds to get the Páez Indigenous people land where they can build homes, cultivate, and once again regain their identity as a tribe. Many of you remember their story: the Christian Páez community displaced from their homes due to a volcanic eruption that destroyed their village and then persecuted for their Christian faith by the leaders of their tribe. Abandoned and left without homes and government aid, they have waited in horrible living conditions for years praying that God would give them a chance to start over.

Thanks to Voice of the Martyrs (VOM) Finland who raised enough money to purchase the land, finally this last 31st of October the families moved onto their new farm. Sammy and I traveled to Cauca to witness the miracle, as the fifty families were able to move out of the shelter camp they were in and onto their new property. We did not know what to expect or how the move would take place. We

imagined that they would move in stages, and as they built their homes, they would move family by family.

Were we ever wrong! Each family took what little belongings they had (mainly stakes and plastic that made up their small huts) and riding on a typical Colombian bus called a *Chiva*, left behind their ghetto. All the families arrived onto their property in one day!

They have no running water (just a stream that passes through the property), no electricity, and no houses as of yet. But no one has ever seen a group of men, women, and children so happy! They seemed like little kids excited to be on a camping trip, when in reality they are facing challenges equal to the old-time settlers claiming the wild western frontier. The first night, most families managed to put a plastic roof over their heads, others slept out in the cold under the stars. They had fires burning, and that first cold night was filled with the warmth of thanks in their eyes and the joy overflowing from their hearts. Sammy and I helped by getting a huge truck full of bamboo logs that they could use to build a temporary camp until the funds come in to build their real houses.

The legal and financial complications prior to the move were immense, and just like when Moses sent the spies into the promised land to scout it out, many said that it could not be done. But a few saw that the land could be claimed, not because they trusted in their own strength but because they knew who would see it through for them, leading them forward with his right arm. The very day before the second payment on the land was made (the payment that ensured their ability to move onto the land), it all seemed very impossible. The land was being purchased from a very difficult lady who turned out later to be heavily involved in witchcraft. When the Christian lawyer who was

negotiating the land found out that
this woman was a witch and that
she was being very difficult with her
demands concerning the land, the
lawyer wanted to quit the deal.

There was so much oppression until
finally Sammy said, "There is no way
that I can believe that one witch is
going to send fifty Christian families
fleeing and deny them the promise
that God has for them! Let's finish this
deal." And so it was done.

Many Christians freak out on
what the world calls Halloween. I've
had friends of mine suggest that we
should keep our children hidden away
so that they won't see all the ghostly
decorations and won't see the other
children dressed up. As if we should
fear those things. But what I have seen
is that we are in a time when whatever
the enemy thinks he owns, God – in
a blink of an eye – reclaims what is
rightfully his. Many Christians have
cowered for decades at the thought

of the "devil's holiday," but I saw the Lord make it his grand celebration.

He took land from a satanic witch and gave it to his people right on Halloween! In Colombia, the 31st of October is called The Day of the Children. And man, this year, it really was!

On this beautiful day of the Lord, he gave homes and a new beginning to over two hundred of his dearly beloved children! And I got to be there to make sure that they had candy to eat while it was happening.

Please help us pray for them during this time. We need the funds and the right people to build their houses and provide them with wells and electricity. The women received a knitting/crochet course last month from our Canadian friends and co-workers and acquired more skills to start their own business. Even though they own the land now, their living conditions are harsh, especially with all the small babies.

But like they have said to us, "First the land. Then the Lord will provide all the rest."

Lisa Stendal-Hernández

PS: One of the things that really impacted me was hearing a kid on the Chiva (bus) singing "...where the Spirit of the Lord is, there is liberty..."

Samuel Hernández

Now, two weeks later and while I was visiting there with friends, Sammy and Lisa showed up once again in Cauca along with Doctor Fernando Torres and his wife, Sol, to see about the health of the Páez community. Fernando and Sol had been our lifelong friends. He was our pediatrician when we were little, and she had always been our dentist. I grew up with Fernando and Sol, and they had been like second parents to me. Sol had always been very direct and blunt with me, and this time was no exception.

Sol asked me if I liked Stephen, and when I said he wasn't my type, she shook her head with disappointment and said, "Well Alethia, you have very bad taste."

Although Lisa and Sammy came with the purpose of helping the Páez community, they also sneakily had the hidden agenda of "helping" me to like Stephen. They praised him and could not help mentioning what a cool and amazing guy he was. Sammy and Lisa have a way of selling things. They had a clothing business for a while, and if someone didn't like an item, by the time they were done with them, Sammy and Lisa would have them convinced it was the coolest piece of clothing ever. I have to say they are good at it.

Up until that time, other than me thinking Stephen was a pleasant guy to be around, I hadn't really thought much more of him. He had told me he came to Colombia to learn Spanish because he wanted to be a translator. A translator? Really? Lame. Poor guy, I was pretty relentless back then. But they tactfully sold me on the idea that he was someone very cool and definitely worth being at least friends with. I soon found out that he was my exact age, and that he actually reminded me of all

my friends in high school. I hadn't had friends my same age since then, and I missed them. So we became really good friends.

In Cauca, we had the club to ourselves, and did we ever enjoy it. We tubed down the waterslide, swam in the lake, played tennis, went canoeing, and even found a yummy ice cream parlor. We became kids again, having fun all day.

Then they lined up a trip for Stephen, Sammy, the doctors, and me to go see the new Páez Indigenous community. When we got there, I was amazed! A sign decorated the entrance of the land with the words "The Goodness of God" in their language and in Spanish. Only two weeks had passed since they had all moved onto their new land, and they had already built a town of the cutest little bamboo houses. It was remarkable to see what they had done with the little that they had and the short amount of time that had passed.

* * *

When our Finnish friends (who sponsored the property) came out to see the land months later, they were moved to tears seeing the gardens they had planted, the houses they had built, and their humble little school and church. One of the Finns said, "We have invested all over the world, in Africa, in Asia, but we have never seen any of that come to fruition like this has."

In fewer than six months, this community had become completely self-sustaining. No other farm I've ever seen here grows such big, juicy, sweet tomatoes, fresh green lettuce, cabbages, carrots, plátanos, and all sorts of other things. Their greenhouses are so well made that they look like the greenhouses one would find on a farm in Canada or Alaska. A friend from North America had recently come to live with them and had taught them how to build these amazing greenhouses. They make and sell their own yogurt, their own coffee, and their own knitting. Every time we visit them, they are sure to fill our car with every crop that is available.

* * *

Doctors Fernando and Sol began checking every child and treating them. They set up a little bamboo hospital room for themselves and worked from it. Sammy and Stephen scouted out the place with Marco Tulio, the Páez's leader.

Meanwhile, I gave the little kids candy. There is a candy factory on the road between our Cauca house and this community, so we always stop by it on our way there to get candy for the kids. I only had one bottle of juice with me, and I gave that to one of the bigger kids. It is amazing how kind and generous these children are with each other. I have never seen anything like it.

Naturally, I thought he would just drink the beverage himself, but instead, he lined all the smaller kids up, and with the cap of the bottle began serving little sips for each one. The little bottle cap passed through each kid as one by one they drank until the bottle was empty. From that moment on, I decided that anything extra I ever had to give would immediately go to them. Fernando called me into his working room and handed me the cutest little baby girl. "Here," he said, passing her to me, "She was named, Alethia, after you."

I walked out just in time to hear Sammy asking Stephen if he could help them build a purifying water system for the village. Stephen had worked for many years in his dad's construction company, building the most beautiful houses in Alaska, and everyone thought he would be a great asset on the team. Stephen said he wasn't too sure because he only had two more months left here, and he needed to focus on studying Spanish. *Lame*, I thought.

We went back to our house later that evening, and Stephen and Isaac began preparing for their trip back to Huila. Stephen had determined in his mind to focus on what he had initially planned to do and study Spanish in the little town where no English-speaking Stendal's roamed.

"You are making the wrong choice," I told him as I walked into the living room where he was sitting.

"Really? Why is that?" he asked.

"Because you need to help these people!"

"Believe me, that Páez community does not need my help. They are amazing!"

"Well, yes they are amazing," I replied, "but that doesn't mean you don't need to help them." It was our first disagreement since he had arrived and I could tell he was not used to getting confronted. In a nicer tone I said, "Look, Thanksgiving is next week. You should come to Bogotá and celebrate it with my family, and then after that, we are all coming out here again and you can help the guys out with this project. You should think about it."

The next morning, he left with Isaac to go to Huila, and a few days later I went back to Bogotá on a plane with Raysa, just in time to celebrate Thanksgiving with my family. My dad's birthday falls around that same time, so it has always been a double celebration and one of our favorite holidays of the whole year.

My mom always cooks the most tender, delicious turkey, mashed potatoes, gravy, stuffing, the whole works! Lisa bakes the best apple and pumpkin pies (using the recipes my great-grandmother used), along with a very special marshmallow fruit salad. And I make the cranberry sauce. At our celebration, it is a tradition for Grandma Pat to tell of how the Lord used Squanto to save the Pilgrims from starving. And then we read the beautiful proclamations that President Abraham Lincoln wrote to honor the holiday.

On the day of our gathering, the doorbell rang, and I went to answer it. To my surprise, it was Stephen with a big smile on his face. We had a wonderful traditional Thanksgiving that night, and a few days later, my whole family was in Cauca again, and the guys were busy building the water purifying system and the electrical wiring for the Páez community.

Me and my dear little Páez friends.

Victor Manuel; my dear little friend.

Chapter 11
Pabel

STEPHEN WAS supposed to stay at my house for one night and then be on his way to fulfill his dream, but two months later, he was still with us. He fit into my world and my family perfectly and ended up spending Christmas with us as well. During this time, we became really good friends.

Many people have come here to help but have ended up doing their own thing once they got here. He came to do his own thing but ended up helping when he saw the needs. It was a lot like the story Jesus tells in the Bible about the son that said no to his father but then did what his father had asked him to do, versus the one that said yes but did not do what his father asked. My family and I came to really respect him. My little brother Russell liked him so much that he asked his friends in Oklahoma to pray that I would like him!

The day after Christmas, Stephen decided he had postponed his dream far too long and

that it was time to go to the small town where no one knew English to learn his Spanish. Off he went to Huila.

Two weeks later, our good friend, Albert Luepnitz, came down from Texas to pray for people. Albert and I met years before at a meeting with ex-generals in Bogotá. After the meeting, he looked at me and asked if I had back problems. To make a long story short, the Lord healed my back when Albert prayed for it and we became good friends.

Even though he was now approaching his 90's, he was still in optimal health conditions. The Lord had given him a genuine gift of healing years before after being paralyzed and getting miraculously healed. Then the Lord gave him a vision of Colombia and Albert knew this was the country he needed to focus on. For thirty years he had been coming down to pray for soldiers wounded in the war, as well as many other people. Sweet, humble and kind; Albert has been another grandfather the Lord has given me on this earth.

My dad usually hosts him by taking him around to different remote areas that need lots of prayer. But Dad was busy because he had to attend to another friend that had come to visit, and it was up to me to take Albert around. I asked dad where I should take him, and he told me to take him wherever the Lord showed me.

The night before Albert arrived, my whole family was going out to eat. I usually go with them, but I was lying in my bed resting, and I was thinking I would get up at any minute to join them. I could hear them getting last-minute things before they went out the door. I tried to get up (and I don't really know if what happened next was merely my imagination or if I was just too tired), but it was as if some powerful, magnificent force was obligating me to stay in bed, literally pressing my body back in bed every time I would make an effort to get up.

I am not the type to miss out on a family outing (ask my sister), but soon I fell into a deep sleep, and in that sleep, I had a dream. I was with my dad and we saw a crippled man on the floor. I turned to Dad and said, "We need to call Albert to pray for him!"

My dad reprovingly said, "Alethia, stop being a Gideon." I woke up and had no clue what the dream meant, although I thought it might be significant.

The next day, Dad drove me to the airport to catch a flight to Huila where I would meet with Albert. I told him about my dream on the drive and asked him why it was wrong to be like Gideon. Dad thought about it and said, "See, Gideon wanted to win the battle with 10,000 men, but God wanted to win it using only 300 men."

It wasn't until a year later that I understood it completely. We were already married, and I told Stephen about my dream and he said, "Alethia, Albert is your army of 10,000, and the Lord would like to win the battle with just you."

Albert and I flew into Neiva, Huila, the southern part of Colombia, where Hugo Tovar Marroquín, a friend of Ernesto and Nenfis, picked us up from the airport. Hugo Tovar was a very experienced lawyer who had helped get Ernesto Pantevis out of prison when he was falsely accused of being an evangelical terrorist. The headlines on the newspapers had been "An Evangelical Pastor Involved in Terrorism."

Ernesto had laughed as he told me the story. He said, "Why would they think I was an evangelical pastor? Nothing could be farther from the truth." Ernesto was a fervent Jew with a sense of humor, and when Hugo Tovar found out that the people who put him in prison were known for being extremely anti-Semitic, he knew it was blatant persecution. He took the case, and Ernesto miraculously got out of prison six months later by the hand of God.

We stayed at Hugo's house the first night, and he took Albert and me all around the city of Neiva to visit every sick person he knew. We went to rich mansions and to the poorest neighborhoods. By the end of our visit, people were so inspired that they were bringing their dogs, cats, and even birds to Albert for prayer. A cat that was limping started walking normally after Albert prayed for it. Then a bird in a cage with a broken wing got better and began flying again. It was amazing to watch all the little animals get healed in the name of the Lord Jesus.

Stephen and Isaac picked us up a day later to drive us down two hours away to Garzón to where Ernesto and Nenfis lived and where Stephen was studying Spanish. I decided to take Albert to that area of the country because so many special friends lived there, including my very close friend Pabel.

* * *

Sadly, Pabel was brutally murdered only nine months after we visited him. Two men from the Páez Nasa Indigenous tribe hung him on a tree using the weight of the Bibles he often carried in his backpack to hand out to people.

Pabel was the kindest person I ever knew. He was my good friend. Pabel came to know about us when one day he listened to a sermon on the radio and knew in his heart that this was the true message he had been searching for his whole life. He decided he needed to meet us, so one Sunday, after a twelve-hour bus ride, he arrive at our meeting in Bogotá with a huge sack of oranges on his back and a smile that covered his face from ear to ear. After this, we went to visit him and his family, and so it happened to be the beginning of a wonderful friendship.

Only a few months before he died, he wrote me the following letter that showed his heart:

My friend Jimeno and I were asking the Lord, "Why are we so alone when we follow you? We look around and friends we used to have, have run off as if we had a serious disease, and we feel the coldness of being lonely."

"It is because you are seeking my friendship," the Lord responded, "I have also had very few friends. Consider Enoch, alone in the midst of so many people. Remember Noah and his family, that first world perished in the water. Remember Joseph. Remember Moses who crossed a desert alone to have my friendship. Think about Elijah, Samuel, David, Isaiah, Jeremiah, and Daniel. Remember my Son and the friends of my Son. With only those few, the Word that you

have today in your hands was written because of the truth of their testimony and because they loved not their lives unto death, sealing them with his blood."

That response into my heart left me stunned.

Many churches claimed to have the Lord, but we didn't feel the Lord in those places. But when the radio exploded with the sound of a preaching that night after I hooked it up high on a tree, the Lord told us directly and said, "These are my true friends." And we both believed it immediately.

Since I was a little boy, I observed the religious people and saw they were very good at speaking pious lies and were almost never careful with the truth.

When the Lord told me, "These are my true friends," I didn't doubt it because I comprehended that the Lord is more of a friend to some than to others. That is something I learned when I was twelve. I decided to always say the truth to my parents, without caring about the consequences, even though I didn't know the Lord. Even if I was in the biggest problem, my answer was always, "Yes, it was me. I did it."

And I practiced this until for me saying a lie was a terror. I kept like this in school, and because of the truth I was the most terrible nerd to my companions. I would hear their loud, mocking and demeaning laughs. It was then that I found out that lies are funny and always find a good audience everywhere.

But I didn't give up, because for me, it meant always being in peace. My motto was that I would rather have any other problem not having to do with lies. I began to realize that vanity is the costume of lies, and that the truth speaks in silence. Lies speak with a lot of bustle and flattery. Because of this, I only had one friend in school. It

wasn't easy to have many, because they would lie to your own face, and that has always been tragic to me. In work I hardly had any friends because sincere people weren't to be found.

So when the Lord spoke to me and said, "These are my true friends," I simply understood that the Lord's friends are also very selected and very few. One day I picked up the Bible and I understood that the Lord loves the truth in the depths, and the Lord is sincere with those who are sincere, and that he shares his most intimate plans with those that love the truth in the depths of their hearts.

To be friends with the few friends that the Lord has in "The Voice of your Conscience" [the name of one of our radio stations], to be able to finally see the truth in people, the friends of the Son, is to my heart an oil of joy in fullness.

Thank you for your prayers, Alethia, my friend.

For many years, he was the one in the limelight, for he was the one God chose to use in that area, but his death opened the door for his wife, Kelly, to become the main character in God's story there in Huila.

Pabel always had a heart for everyone. He wanted everyone to know God and his immeasurable love for us, so Pabel prayed continually that these violent Indigenous groups would change and see the love of God. When he was killed, the governor of the tribe asked Kelly to come and dictate a sentence for the two murderers.

These tribes have their own legal system, and since she was the one affected, they thought it was only natural to unite her with the killers and have her give the verdict. Many more people from the tribe came to this meeting, including the governor and the two murderers. They were sitting in a circle, and Kelly later described being so angry with these men that she wanted to get up and strangle them, punch them, hit them, and yell, "Why did you do this to me!? Why

would you leave me without a husband, my kids without a father?!"

She didn't know what she wanted to do to them, but when the time came for her to choose their punishment, she got up from her chair, and as she slowly walked toward her adversaries, not knowing where her rage would take her, she heard a clear voice calm her spirit that said, "The same nature that caused them to kill your husband is in you."

At that moment, she knew she had to forgive them, but she did not think she could. She told me that it must have been something supernatural, something from her heavenly Father, something that was definitely not in her, because instantly her anger turned, and when she finally reached the chairs where the murderers of her husband were sitting, she could only cry and say to them, "I forgive you."

The governor and the entire tribe saw Kelly forgive her husband's murderers. Now there is a beautiful awakening taking place over there as I write this story. But Kelly's adventures with that tribe are another account. Pabel's death made the way for it all to happen. Truly, the blood of a martyr is the seed that is planted for a whole new harvest. Only sometimes you wish it didn't have to be that particular seed. The choice comes from the Lord of the Harvest alone.

* * *

I wanted Albert and Stephen to meet Pabel. So on one of our days there, Albert, Stephen, Ernesto, and I drove two hours away to the little farm where Pabel and his family lived. Pabel met us halfway, and while he led us on his little motorcycle, he would stop and move all the big rocks out of way so that our little car could pass unscathed.

Albert gave Stephen his little video camera and told Stephen to record every miracle he saw. As Stephen saw miracle after miracle, he began to remember the promise he had made God years before. Being in a spiritual desert where he saw many pastors that weren't leading the people right, he promised God that if he ever did meet a true disciple of Jesus, he would drop everything and give his life over to the Lord. Albert was the disciple

God showed him. From then on, he made a truly radical decision, one that would change his life forever. He decided to follow the Lord Jesus with all of his heart.

Pabel, Kelly and their two kids: Israel David and Linda Estefanía.

Chapter 12
Finding Home

ONLY A FEW days after Albert and I left Huila, Stephen had to head back to Bogotá to renew his visa and told Ernesto he would only be gone a couple of days. Ernesto said, "No you won't. I had a dream that you left, and you kept on trying to come back but a strong hand wouldn't let you come. You won't be back for a very long time."

Stephen didn't think much of it, but it ended up happening. (We were finally able to go back to visit Ernesto in Huila years after we were married.) We kept trying to go, but something always happened to stop us.

Meanwhile, Stephen came to Bogotá with only a few of his things packed, thinking he would surely go back to Huila in two or three days. But my astute mom asked him to please remodel the library in her house and the recording studio. This took him three months of work, in which he had to stay with us. By the end of his time doing that, my dad

invited him to go to Africa along with my two brothers to see about the purchase of a radio station over there.

Stephen went to Africa with them for three weeks, and when he came back, he started telling me about his trip. Usually I would have stayed up to listen, but this time he scared me.

He was talking like someone who is getting a glimpse of something bigger than themselves. I had always heard my dad talk like this, but very few other people inspired me this way. This is something I had always looked for in someone, and I had never seen it before in Stephen, until then.

I excused myself by saying I was tired. I went up to my room. He was getting to my heart, and I didn't want him there.

I had always found him a comforting presence to be around, but it had never felt as it did now. Something about Stephen had changed, and I could sense it, though I did not know exactly what it was because he never told me anything about what had happened in Huila or about his promise to God.

My mom knew I was a tough nut to crack, so she invited Stephen out to eat one night and gave him a little piece of advice. Though she didn't mention my name she told him, "Some things in life come easy, but the best things in life are worth fighting for."

At the end of May, we went to a marimba concert with some friends. After the night of listening to fun music was over and he took me back to my house, we hugged. And that was it. I felt as if I had come home for the first time in my life.

Chapter 13
The Proposal

SOON CAME what might be one of the greatest battles I have ever had to go through. So many doubts about Stephen crept into my mind that I would break up with him every time I had the chance. Sometimes it was up to two or three times a day. I was like the girl in the movie *50 First Dates* who had amnesia and had to be re-won every day. But it was during this time that Stephen proved he was made for me. Day after day, he won me over by being sweet and kind.

One day he told me to take my dog Lucy out, and when I came back, he had made a desk for me, and had positioned it right where I could see the city so I could find more inspiration as I wrote the book called *The Hidden Agenda*.[6]

---

6 Russell M. Stendal and Alethia Stendal, The Hidden Agenda, Published by Ransom Press International.

Then he would bring me all sorts of treats as I was working, just to keep me going. And whenever I broke up with him, all he would do was smile and say that he loved me and was here for me, and that he would wait as long as it took.

None of my crazy girl fits ever scared him enough to leave me. By the time I finished writing my first book, we were married, and I dedicated the first copy to him saying:

To the most wonderful husband anyone could ever have. I love you. Thank you for helping me be honest in every single page. Thank you for telling me how to be kinder to people in the way I portrayed them. You truly helped me let my real self shine. Thank you for providing the desk with the view of the city in which this book came to life. Thank you for bringing me treats while I was writing, and for finding a way to calm me down when the editors or others would mess up the text, or when my dad would get intense about it. I couldn't have finished it without

you, and to think we even had time to
get married three times along the way!
I love you.

It was the beginning of June in the year
2014 when we began dating, and the soccer
World Cup was on in full force; Colombia
was one of the best teams in the competition.
Two weeks after we told my whole family
we were dating, he decided to propose to
me. Colombia was playing against Uruguay,
and Stephen told his dad that night that if
Colombia won, he would propose.

My brothers had the camera aimed at us
during the whole game (Stephen had asked
them to record) and of course Colombia won
2–0. We were jumping up and down, yelling
at the top of our lungs for the victory. Then
Stephen got on one knee and my brother
brought in the camera closer to us, and just as
he was reaching into his pocket for the ring, I
said in disgust, "No, stop. Don't do that!"

I didn't know he was proposing. I thought
he was pretending to be a dwarf. The night
before he had been doing this joke about
being a dwarf and walking on his knees

everywhere. What did he expect me to think when he got on his knees once again the next day?

I found out later that Stephen was devastated because he thought I was telling him not to propose to me. He called my sister who was in Cauca and asked her what he should do. She gave him ideas. They could not figure out what had happened. Lisa said maybe I didn't like the idea of having everyone watching, so she suggested making it a bit more private.

Meanwhile I was thinking "What's taking him so long to propose?"

The very next day my mom, Stephen, and I took a flight to Cauca where my sister was. I took the window seat where I was given a first-class view of the beautiful sunset that was before us. Stephen sat next to me in the middle seat, and mom took the aisle seat. On one side of the window, thunder and lightning filled the skies, with the sunset creating the beautiful colors of orange and pink right behind the storm. On the other side of the horizon, there was a sliver of the new moon

with a bright, magnificent star that looked just like a giant diamond beside it. The blue and light purple sky behind it made the star look even brighter. I turned to my mom and said, "Look mom, it's the new moon, with the star right next to it!"

I didn't know it right then, but my mom looked at it and, on the verge of tears, went to the bathroom to cry. Stephen had told my mom that he was planning on proposing to me on that flight, and she had remembered something I had said to her months before on the night when my friends Ángela and Salomón got married in Cauca. The night was clear, and the only thing that could be seen was the little sliver of the new moon beginning to grow again and the bright diamond-looking star right next to it. That night I turned to my mom and said, "When I get engaged, I want the sky to be lit like that."

This was only a few months before I started dating Stephen, but back then I didn't even like him and definitely had no thoughts about

marrying him. I thought some other guy
would come to sweep me off my feet.

My mom remembered this, and when she
saw me point to that moon and that star, she
could barely control her tears enough to get to
the bathroom.

Contorting himself in a sick manner,
Stephen pretended he had a stomachache
and called for medicine. The flight attendant
came quickly with a cup of water and a packet
of *sal de frutas*, something similar to Alka-
Seltzer. Stephen hunched over as if in pain,
and handed me the water and the packet and
asked me to help him prepare the medicine.
When I opened the packet, I felt a lump that
would not come out. I reached into it with my
fingers and brought out the most beautiful,
perfectly cut diamond set in a rose gold ring.

I couldn't believe how lovely it was and
how it fit my ring finger perfectly.

Seven months before, when Stephen had
first arrived, he had a ring on his pinky, and
I absent-mindedly asked him for it and put
it on my ring finger. We had barely met, yet

he noticed that his ring fit my ring finger perfectly. And he had remembered.

The funny thing is that when I put his ring on my ring finger, I remember thinking, "I shouldn't have done that. I hope he doesn't think I'm one of those crazy girls hinting at something."

"Alethia, will you marry me?" Stephen interrupted my thoughts, suddenly sounding a lot better from his "stomach ache".

But I was so in awe of the ring on my finger that the question slipped to the back of my mind, and I also thought I didn't need to answer such an obvious question. Of course I wanted to marry him. Must I state the obvious?

A few moments later, I turned my head to see that Stephen was looking at me expectantly. I had already rejected the poor guy's proposal once, and my deficiency in answering his question now was probably killing him. I looked at him for the first time since I put the ring on, smiled, and said, "Yes!"

My mom was watching the whole thing and taking pictures. Then we opened a bottle of wine and had a toast on the flight.

When we got to the house in Cauca, we sat down to talk, and I asked Stephen for the first time since I had met him what his name meant. "Crowned one," he said. "It's Greek."

And suddenly the man I had met in Ketchikan almost six years before and what he had told me flooded my mind again, "Alethia, God has given you a crown. You need to cherish it and not give it to the wrong man. The right man will respect you."

Right after the proposal.

Chapter 14

Our Lake Wedding

July 12, 2014, Villa de Leyva, Colombia

I HAD ALWAYS dreamed of getting married on the beach on Colombia's northern coast in Parque Tayrona, near the city of Santa Marta. It is a breathtaking beach surrounded by the Sierra Nevadas, the tallest mountain range near the ocean on this side of the hemisphere. This is where my grandparents have their work with the Kogi Indigenous tribe. Because of this, I had spent long periods of my childhood there, and I loved it. A few years before, my family had gone camping in this stunning oasis. On the trip I got a stomach bug from the food and the water that sent me to bed for weeks. Despite the bad memory, I still had the dream of getting married there.

Another time, we went back to that same place and my whole family got sick for weeks, again because of the food. Lisa thought she was going to die, and my brother Dylan got hepatitis B. I got so sick for the next three months that I could hardly do anything and ended up getting hospitalized in Orlando, Florida, because my appendix ruptured, infecting all my organs.

So, even though the ocean did sound amazing, I did not want to risk poisoning all my wedding guests or the possibility of not enjoying a honeymoon because I might be too sick. I quietly set that lifelong wedding destination plan aside.

My next dream was getting married near one of those crystal-clear blue lakes in Minnesota that I loved swimming in so much. Providentially, months before, I had discovered another beautiful clear blue lake, just as pretty as the ones in Minnesota – maybe even more so because desert and mountains surrounded it. This lake was near Villa de Leyva, a quaint, picturesque little town paved with huge stones that was located about three hours from Bogotá; my family loves to visit there from time to time.

After the beach, this was my next best choice, and my favorite restaurant with the

finest oven-smoked ribs was there. This food, I knew, would not poison anyone because I had eaten there a lot.

In a conversation with my father and Stephen, I said that a good time to have the wedding would be the end of February. In my mind, it would give us about seven months to plan everything, and Stephen's family and friends would have enough time to be able to attend. It seemed perfect. Except that my dad was not in agreement with me at all.

For twenty-seven years, I had grown up with a dad who my friends marveled at because he gave me so much freedom. He seldom gave his opinion to me about anything or told me what I should or should not do. I only had his example, and whenever I asked what he thought I should do in a certain situation, he would always say, "You need to hear from the Lord for yourself. What is he saying to you?" It is a lot harder to get on your knees and ask the Lord for direction, rather than being told what to do by someone else.

However, once in a while he did have a very strong opinion for me about something and I had learned to give his suggestions careful consideration.

For example, before I went to the US with Lisa and all our friends for a tour of the movie we had just filmed, he told me blatantly, "Don't go. This is not your trip."

"How do you know it isn't my trip?" I asked him.

"I just know. This is not your trip, sweetie."

But I was a big girl in my mid-twenties, and I was determined to go. Only a week after I left, my appendix ruptured at Disney World and sent me to the hospital. The doctor who operated on me in Florida had said I was a living miracle. That was most certainly not my trip. The same thing would have probably happened had I stayed in Colombia, but I would have gone to the hospital sooner because here I have medical insurance. Also my body would not have gone through so much poisoning.

The other occasion when my dad had a strong opinion for me was in relation to

going on that trip to Alaska to help drive my grandparents. He said the trip was important and that I should go. I would not be the same person I am now if I hadn't gone.

Now he had another strong suggestion for me, "Don't wait until February," he said. "If it is in your hearts to get married, do it as soon as possible."

"Why?" I asked him.

"Anything could happen by the time February comes around. We might be in a completely different deal by then," he answered.

It was true. With the way things went in my family and in our work, one never knew what was around the corner.

"Okay, we'll get married sooner, if that's what you think, Dad." (Little did I know what would happen in February.)

But back to the wedding. Mom and I soon learned that Stephen's visa for Colombia was about to expire and that he could not merely get it stamped for another three months like he had before. He had already used that option twice and could not legally do it again.

This time, he would have to leave the country for six months before returning again – unless he married a Colombian girl in less than two weeks. This moved the wedding date even sooner than we had planned. All of the notaries we could find in Bogotá were booked for months in advance. Finally, I thought of calling a friend of ours that used to own a notary, Jorge Castellanos. He was also the one who married Lisa and Sammy years before. I asked him to please ask the notary in Villa de Leyva to marry us in ten days. He said he would call the judge, and "put in a word for us," and then I could call him up. I called the judge twenty minutes later, and he said he had an opening to marry us for July 12. Stephen's visa expired July 15. It was perfect.

Marthica Hernández, mom and I rushed to a mall to buy my wedding dress. The very first one I tried on was *perfect*. I was so blessed to have been able to pick out one of my wedding dresses with these two very special ladies: my mom and Marthica, another maternal figure the Lord has given me. With the most important item of the event in

the bag, Mom, Stephen, and I flew back to
Bogotá to arrange the rest of the details.

Ten days later, we were in Villa de Leyva
to celebrate with twenty of my closest friends
and family. We all stayed in the quaintest
little white cabins at the edge of the town.
The morning of the wedding, my cousin
Raysa, who is a make-up and hair artist, gave
me her magic touch. Then my immediate
family, Stephen, cousin Raysa, and I headed
for the notary in the center of town.

The judge recited everything we needed to
know about marriage and made sure we knew
what we were getting into. Then we both
signed our names and were pronounced husband and wife.

After that, we went to a waffle place that
I really like, and everyone else was waiting
for us with big smiles and hugs. We had a
delicious breakfast and took pictures in that
special, quaint restaurant. Then we walked
over to a hill in the middle of the vast,
beautiful desert, where my dad and Aníbal
Hernández (the other father God has given
me on this earth and Marthica's husband)

each said a beautiful prayer for me and Stephen in our new marriage. Many are the times the Lord has proven that he does hear the prayer of these two very special people in my life.

After the prayer, Stephen disappeared for a little while. Just when I was beginning to wonder where he had gone, he appeared with a beautiful wreath he had just made with freshly picked flowers. He placed the wreath on my head and my sister took a picture. That was the cherry on top of my cake.

After that we all went to the magical, clear-blue lake I had found – the one that reminded me of the magnificent lakes in Minnesota. There, we had a lovely little picnic with smoked cheese, bread, and wine.

In the evening, Lisa took amazing pictures of us in our wedding attire in the scenic little white town with the pebbled stones. The scenery worked perfect with my white knee-length, country-style wedding dress and cowboy boots.

We made reservations in my favorite restaurant, (the one with the mouth-watering smoked baby back ribs,) where we all feasted.

The restaurant (known for their delicious cakes) made us two: an apple streusel and banana fudge! Everyone made a toast to us. Some of our friends made us laugh, and others made us cry.

I was never a big fan of tradition. I never wanted to walk down an aisle. I had always felt very awkward walking down the aisle as a bridesmaid and didn't want to do it as a bride. My dream was to make my own tradition. I wanted to enjoy a whole day with only my closest friends and family. So for me, this was perfect.

I bought a dress for Lisa – my maid of honor – and for my flower girl, Gabriella – two very special people in my life. I had found Lisa's dress on a trip I had gone on with her previously. Her favorite color is green, and this was such a special green dress, perfect for a desert wedding; it was also knee-length and looked great with her cowboy boots. Gaby wore a short white dress, similar to mine, also with cowboy boots.

We had a wonderful day. Now the only thing missing was the wedding reception. When Dad first heard we were dating, he had bought Stephen and me first class tickets to Alaska with some miles he had left over; this trip was scheduled for the month of August so I could meet Stephen's family and his family could meet me. It was already the 12th of July, and I wanted a wedding reception before going to Alaska in August.

The only one who could possibly pull off a reception in less than three weeks was Lisa. My wonderful sister, talented in so many ways, including the making of weddings and events, had already begun to plan a great celebration for me, but since the only available dates for the event fell on a weekend where my dad could not be there, I had cancelled it.

In Villa de Leyva, I told my dad about my decision to cancel it because he would not be there, and he gave me the idea of scheduling it a few days before then, so it would fall on a Thursday instead of a Saturday.

"I'll be there all Thursday; my flight doesn't leave till midnight on that day," he said.

It had never occurred to me to celebrate during a weekday. "But I already told Lisa to cancel it."

"Don't worry, your mom and I will talk to her." Dad was my ally during this whole wedding madness, and in my experience, if he supported something, it would happen without a shadow of a doubt.

I had always dreamed of having my reception be like a talent show where all my friends could get up, recite poetry, sing songs, dance, or play music. I wrote my sister a letter telling her everything I wanted. I wanted popcorn, cupcakes, candy, and a great show. I wanted Óscar Arias to sing at my reception. I wanted Dad, Fernando Torres, and Aníbal Hernández to give a speech for us.

Lisa, along with Alex, our good friend and co-worker, did an excellent job planning this in no time. And of course, Lisa met every requirement on the list.

My family put on the show of a lifetime. It felt like Bilbo Baggins's 111th birthday party, only better![7]

---

7 From The Fellowship of the Ring, the first volume of

There was everything from singing, to dances, and music recitals. Songs were written and performed for us. Special poetry was written and recited in our honor. My cousin's from my mom's side danced to a special sort of folk music from the Eastern Plains of Colombia called *joropo*, featuring the harp as the main instrument. They also played a concert with the mandolin. Anyone who grows up on that side of the country is taught from a very early age how to dance *joropo* and how to play all the instruments in it. It was (to say the least) a very professional rendition of the wonderful music that defines that region where my mom is from. My favorite *mariachi* singer, Óscar Arias, came and performed for us with his whole band. He even wrote a song in our honor.

My dad, Aníbal Hernández, and Fernando Torres (all important figures in my life) each got up and gave us a very special speech. César Trigos, a special friend of our family, wrote us a song and played it with his guitar.

The Lord of the Rings, and the scene of Bilbo Baggins's eleventy-first (111th) birthday.

My siblings and friends made a movie in which they acted out Stephen and me and all the funny stories that happened during the time we were dating. Fercho, Alex, and Lisa, my three friends and co-workers, got up and announced every single presentation as if they were hosting the Oscars. The three of them are great actors.

Lisa also baked me the yummiest vanilla cupcakes (my favorite) and decorated them with all my favorite colors; she had the red vintage popcorn machine we had used in all our movie premiers throughout the countryside set up and working, and all my favorite candy was placed on each table.

I got to enjoy every detail because I had not been stressed out planning it. It is like when you bake a cake and eat it; sometimes you don't enjoy it as much because you've tasted too much of the batter beforehand. It's much different when someone else bakes you a cake and you haven't tasted it yet, and *then* you eat it. I personally enjoy that cake much more.

I don't think anyone could ever have had such a fun and entertaining wedding reception. We were loved, and we were in love.

My beautiful flowered wreath.

Chapter 15

Our Alaskan Wedding

Sunday, August 17, 2014, Fairbanks, Alaska

SOON AFTER Stephen proposed, we wrote to his dad and told him all about us. Papa Miller wrote back immediately and said, "How about we make you a wedding up here in Alaska on the seventeenth of August?"

It was meant to be. The date, August 17, falling on a Sunday and being located in Alaska were important details to me: it was the same date that fell on exactly the same day of the week that the man in Ketchikan, Alaska, heard a word directly from God for me, exactly six years before. "The right man will respect you."

Stephen had showed me the meaning of the word *respect* in every single way. Respect means even more than I had ever thought it meant. Respect means embracing and cherishing everything that I am, everything I represent, and everything I am a part of:

my country, my family, our work, and most importantly, the Lord himself.

Stephen told me his dad's idea, and I said yes without hesitating, so long as my whole family could go and my dad was the one marrying us. Dad walked by and overheard us talking about it; "A wedding in Alaska?" he asked.

I said, "Yes, Stephen's family would like to have a wedding for us up there."

A few days before this, I had been talking to Stephen about what my new last name would be. Jokingly, I said, "Miller? I'd rather go with your mom's side of the family and take the name Underhill; it's cool, just like Frodo's last name, Underhill, in *The Lord of the Rings*." Dad walked by just in time to hear this last part of the conversation.

"Underhill?" he said in surprise, "Stevie, are you an Underhill?"

"Yes, I am."

"So, you are related to Jay Underhill?"

"She was my grandmother," Stephen replied.

Stunned, Dad said, "Jay was a dear friend of mine. She was one of my top three favorite people. Anything that the Lord has given me is yours too." This last phrase, he spoke with conviction.

Stephen's grandmother Jay and his grandpa Dave were also lifelong friends of my grandparents, and every time they drove up to Delta Junction, Alaska, they would park their motorhome in Dave and Jay's yard for a few days. I had vague memories of both sets of Stephen's grandparents but never any of *him*. We must have met back when we were little kids, because my mom remembered seeing him – a tanned, wild Alaskan boy with his dog. And Stephen's mom remembered our family coming to speak at their church.

So now as we talked about getting married in Alaska and Dad overheard it, he said, "Let's look for tickets right now," and went into his office. Dad has never been one to leave things for the next day. Once he gets excited about something, beware. "Okay sweetie, what are the dates?" And so I told him. "Who do you want to have go? Just me and your mom?"

"No dad. I want the whole family to go: mom, Bubba, Dylan, Sammy, Lisa, Jack and Gaby...everyone. Or else I simply won't get married up there."

"Okay, we'll see what we can do." He looked into it, and for some reason there were extremely low prices for those dates. By 1:00 a.m. he had used all his personal savings and had purchased the tickets for our family.

"Well, I had ten thousand dollars saved for something; I didn't know exactly what," he said, as he smiled and pushed the purchase button on the computer.

Stephen's family planned a beautiful wedding for us with lots of good food and a delicious vanilla cake with lemon filling, decorated with wildflowers, topped with Alaskan blueberries. Natural-born chefs of the best kind make up his family, and they all brought something to share.

Most people have merely okay food at their weddings (because caterers for such an event care more about the presentation than the actual content) and an okay-tasting cake, but oh my! This food was amazing and so was the

cake. I can honestly say that all of my three wedding celebrations had the most yummy, delicious cakes and heartwarming food. My Alaskan cousins and sisters and aunts brought tons of scrumptious cookies and deserts to share.

To remind me a little bit of home, we put Colombian music on the whole time.

Besides my family, I had two very special guests: one was my soul sister and good friend, Melissa Almario; the other was Albert Luepnitz. I had him to thank for many things in my life, including my husband. Most of the other people were from Stephen's family, since I had already had a wedding with my friends and my extended family. Still, there were a lot of people, given that Stephen seems to be related to half of Alaska.

It was a traditional wedding in many ways, but I found that being traditional was very nice after all.

My bridal gown was long, delicate, and gold. A beautiful light, translucent, bridal coat that my sister had worn for her wedding went over the dress. Lisa was nice enough to lend it to me. Just like my wedding desert dress, this one was also *perfect*. I wore a rose-gold bridal crown, and one of Stephen's cousins curled my hair. Later, Stephen said I had looked like an elf about to float off to another world.

I walked down the aisle of fresh green Alaskan grass to a lighthearted song called "Concerning Hobbits" found in the soundtrack of *The Lord of the Rings*. There at the end, Stephen waited for me, standing by a wooden cedar arch decorated with lovely flowers; he had built it himself the day before.

It was a beautiful sight. Only, Stephen wasn't crying. To give him the benefit of the doubt, perhaps it was because it was already our third wedding. At every wedding I had ever gone to, the man was always crying at the end of the aisle as soon as the bride walked in. I laughed thinking about how unorthodox he was. We looked at each other with big bright smiles as I walked towards him.

We had already said our vows to one another privately on July 7, back in Bogotá,

just a few days before our wedding in Villa
de Leyva. That night, after one of our many
fights, I had decided to wash his feet with
warm water as a gesture of change and
forgiveness, and as I was doing this, I said my
vows to him. I promised to serve him every
day, I told him I would respect him, and I
said that his heart would always be pure in
my eyes. In other words, that I believed in
the work the Lord had done and was doing in
him, and I would never question it. I would
never judge his heart.

We both cried that time and he also said
his vows to me. He said he would always
place God first in his life and me second. Now
we said our vows to each other with all our
friends and family as witnesses. Stephen said
he would place God first and me second, only
this time he said it in a less sentimental way.
When I spoke, I was less emotional too, and
of course I had momentarily forgotten what
my vows had originally been so I said, "I
promise to always place myself in God's hands
because I know that he is the only one who
can enable me to be a good wife to you."

If I was very untraditional, Stephen was even more so. He didn't even know that he had to put the ring on my finger when Dad handed it to him. He just plopped it in my palm as if it were a piece of candy, and I put it on myself.

Dad gave the shortest message I had ever heard him preach, but I still remember what he said.

* * *

In his message, Dad spoke of the wedding at Cana and of how it wasn't the "right time" for Jesus to start his ministry, but he did it anyway at the request of Mary. One of the things that impresses me the most from reading the Bible and especially the Gospels is that people, insignificant people, always change things.

Perhaps that is why I liked *The Lord of the Rings* so much, because it is about little, insignificant people, called hobbits that change the outcome. One of the lines from the movie that always impacted me was when

Lady Galadriel told Frodo, "Even the smallest person can change the course of the future."[8]

It was not the Lord Jesus's time to begin his work, but Mary, his mother, insisted, and so he began his ministry that day. This is found consistently throughout all the Scriptures. Nothing is ever written in stone: little people can, and always do, change the course of the future.

Abigail changed David's mind as he was riding out to battle against her household.

A woman knocked on Jesus's door and asked for help for her demon-possessed daughter. At first his answer was, "It is not good to take the children's bread and to cast it to the little dogs."

But she surprised him by her response when she said, "Yes, Lord, yet the little dogs eat of the crumbs which fall from their masters' table."

"Then Jesus answered and said unto her, O woman, great is thy faith; be it unto thee even as thou desire. And her daughter was made

---

8   J.R.R Tolkien, The Lord of the Rings Trilogy, first published by George Allen and Unwin in 1954-1955

whole from that very hour" (Matthew 15:25-28).

Imagine that this woman was able to change the Lord Jesus's mind, the Son of God!

Another woman simply touched Jesus's garment and virtue came out of his body.

Ruth cleaved to Naomi, her Jewish mother-in-law, thus changing the course of her future. Even though Ruth wasn't an Israelite, she would not let Naomi return to her land without her and courageously said, "Thy people shall be my people, and thy God my God" (Ruth 1:16). Hence she became an indispensable part in the lineage that led all the way up to our Lord Jesus Christ. She was not even Jewish, yet an entire book in the Old Testament is dedicated to telling her story.

Queen Esther may be the greatest example of all. She was able to find grace in the eyes of the king and convince him not to slay all the Jews without first giving them a chance to defend themselves, therefore saving her whole race from imminent extermination.

No other history book has ever contained so many examples of women changing the course of the future, no matter what their

background was. Women were the littlest, most insignificant people back then, yet they altered the outcome of history when they found grace in the eyes of God.

Dad ended the ceremony by saying that in order to be part of what God was doing, we had to forgive. It is such a simple statement, but so full of truth.

* * *

This was our last wedding and we had waited to start our honeymoon until the end of the ceremony in Alaska.

The gifts we received that day were enough to give us a five-star honeymoon in Alaska's best accommodations for the remaining three weeks of our stay. We took a road trip up to the coast, visited the most beautiful little towns by the ocean, and stayed in the best hotels. The extraordinary thing is that in every new town we went to, it was as if we had some designated purpose from the Lord to be there.

Our honeymoon gave us friends that I believe were meant to be, seeing as Stephen and I are not the kind of people who are prone to or even good at making friends with random people. But in every town or hotel where we stopped, we met someone special; that someone would tell someone else, and soon we would have a crowd of people listening to our story, and all the other stories we had about Colombia and all our adventures together.

We were like that couple I had met in Ketchikan years ago, telling everyone the tale of how it all happened. And our audience was like I had been then– taking it all in, wishing that one day the good Lord would intervene in my life too. I don't mean to say that God has the same plan for everyone. One thing that Aníbal told me when I was single was, "Whether or not God gives you a husband is up to him. What you have to decide is whether or not you will follow him, with or without a husband, with or without children. Whether his will is for you to be alone or to be accompanied throughout it all, what will you do?"

Once again, I am reminded of the story of the lost prince in the *Chronicles of Narnia*

book *The Silver Chair* by C.S. Lewis. "Courage friends," came Prince Rillian's voice, "whether we live or die, Aslan will be our good lord."[9]

I had several things I wished to see: one was the northern lights and the other was a bear. One night, we stopped at a cabin that had a great view of a lake. As soon as it got dark, the beautiful, emerald green northern lights showed up and began dancing right in front of our window. As we were driving out of there the next day, I thought, "That was so nice of the Lord to show me the northern lights once again in full summer" – something that was rare and usually only happened in the dead of winter. "Now the only thing I have left to see is a bear." Only seconds after I thought this, a black bear came running out from the bushes and stood right in front of our car!

9   C. S. Lewis, The Silver Chair (1953), published by
Geoffrey Bles p.187

Chapter 16

The Importance of Lucy

THERE COULD not be any two human beings that are more different from each other than my parents are. Dad can be alone, working for hours, days, and even weeks on end. Mom needs company. Dad likes traveling and talking to new people. Mom would rather stay at home. Dad is the most focused person on earth. His incredible ability to focus is the reason why he has written more than twenty books in the past five years and edited two Bibles – one in English and one in Spanish – in less than a decade. Mom, well she is sort of scatter-brained, in that sense making her a great mom because she is always thinking of a new plan, whether it's going to the river for a swim, making fish for dinner, or visiting Grandma. Let's just say it never gets boring when she is around. Dad is a dog lover. Mom is not a dog lover (or so she says).

Dad and Lisa (the dog lover of my siblings) had been trying to get us to have a dog in the house for the longest time, but of course my mom had put her foot down on numerous occasions and never allowed it to happen. We had had a series of dogs previously that would last a matter of months in our house before they were shipped off by mom to her brother's house in the country. There was no talking mom into getting a dog, no matter how many times Dad and Lisa would try. Until one day the two dog lovers of the family left on a trip to the USA, and my two little brothers, mom, and I were left to take care of things alone.

On one of those Saturdays in which the house was cleaned up, lunch had already been served, and there was not much else to do, we decided to put a movie on. The movie we chose was *I Am Legend* starring Will Smith. It is a terribly tragic speculative film about everyone on earth dying of a virus. By the end of the movie, the only ones left are Will Smith and

his female German shepherd. This dog was so faithful to him that it was heart-wrenching. She was the only companion he had left when his whole family had died with the virus. The power of this dog's character in the movie was so strong that by the time the credits rolled, the four of us (even mom) had decided we desperately needed a dog – a girl dog.

Five minutes after the movie ended, we were all in the car heading for the pet store. They had just sold a litter of golden retriever puppies and there was only one female puppy left, presumably the only one left because she may have been the runt. The first thing she did when she saw us was pounce from side to side in a playful way. My brother Russell and I knew as soon as we saw her trying to play with us that she was the one we wanted. There was no questioning it, no looking for another pet store. We took her home immediately in a little cardboard box. We called her Lucy, who is also a character in the *Chronicles of Narnia* book series.

We wrapped Lucy up in a box with a ribbon on it to surprise Dad and Lisa when they arrived at the airport. Were they ever surprised! This time, the dog lovers had nothing to do with the new household dog. Mom had bought her. Hence, (to Lucy's great fortune, as well as ours), she would be protected from getting shipped off to my uncle's house, for the rest of her life.

Lucy lived a good three years and then one Christmas got terribly sick. The Christmas festivities were not enough to calm the pain we each felt for Lucy. For Christmas Eve we all went to visit my aunt and uncle's farm for the weekend, but my brother Russell stayed home to take care of her. Lucy was bleeding internally. Russell nursed her back to health. Even on Christmas night, he did not celebrate; he slept by her side and made sure to give her the medications every ten minutes. She was at risk of dying of dehydration. God answered our prayers that Christmas, and Lucy was back to her normal playful self in a matter of weeks.

We had a nice healthy dog for another three or four years, until one day we discovered a tumor growing in her forehead. We went to check it with the vet, and he

said it was the result of a tooth infection. We treated her "tooth infection," but the tumor kept growing. Around this same time, I got engaged to Stephen.

Only one month after we got back from our honeymoon in Alaska, we had to put Lucy to sleep because the tumor had overtaken her face, and her eye was now bulging out. No amount of prayer or medication healed her this time. Lucy had been with us for seven and a half years, but it was time for her journey with us to end.

Fortunately, I was not in town when we made the decision to put her to sleep. I don't think I could have gone through with it. When I got back home, there was no Lucy wagging her tale and whining with joy to greet me at the door. My heart was broken. I asked my dad why it was that God did not make dogs live as long as humans did. Why was their life so short in comparison? My dad told me the Lord designed it that way so that we could have a practice round. In life we will have to face the death of loved ones at some point, and sometimes God gives us a dog first, just so we are more prepared for the time when we will have to say goodbye to our parents, to our siblings, or to our spouse.

For weeks, when I would go to bed at night, a thought of Lucy would cross my mind and it would send me into inconsolable tears. Stephen did his best to calm me, but even his embrace and kind words could not make the sadness go away.

Until one night, when the thought of Lucy came into my mind again, and I was about to burst into my usual bout of nightly tears, I made up my mind to do something different. This time, instead of wallowing in my pain, I began to honestly thank the Lord for the time Lucy had been here with us. I thanked him for letting us have such a beautiful dog in the first place. I thanked him because he was taking way better care of her than I ever did. I thanked him because of how I imagined her to be right at that minute. I imagined her running freely through fresh green grass and beautiful flowers, happy and free, instead of being confined to our small apartment in a very polluted city. She was a happy dog in my

dreams – happier than she ever was here. That night the sadness left me. Gratefulness had proven to be the most wonderful remedy.

Chapter 17

The Play

October 2014, Bogotá, Colombia

WE HAD ONLY been married for a few months and Lisa had just finished writing a play in Spanish called *La Máquina* – which means "the machine" – and she wanted Stephen to design and build the set and for me to be the costume designer and an actress in it. I got the part of Doña Antonia, an eighty-year-old maid.

This play was based on a hilariously true story that happened to Grandma Pat back when she was in her thirties, during the time when she and B-pa lived in the Eastern Plains of Colombia. Grandma had always told the story to us growing up, and every single time she would tell it, we would all die laughing. Lisa played "Donna," who in reality was supposed to be Grandma.

We had to rent a theater a few blocks away from our house in order to be able to have

practices and have a place to present it in the beginning of December. When I walked into the theater for the very first time to rehearse the lines with the rest of the cast, I didn't like the feeling I got from the place at all. It felt dark to me. Lisa and Daniela Atiencia (my high school buddy and the director of the play) went to check out another play that was showing in that theater, and they said it was extremely degrading. They were hoping they might see an example of a good production, but I wasn't surprised when they didn't. For some reason, most theater and film productions are very dark here in Bogotá. Theater is a powerful weapon that, if used for good, could be amazing. But as far as I've seen, it hasn't been used for good because people write what is in their hearts, and if all that is in there is darkness, well that's what you'll get.

Walking into that theater reminded me of all the times I had walked into film schools looking for a place to study.

* * *

When I graduated from high school, I knew I wanted to be a filmmaker, and my dad told me that I could either go to film school or instead, use the college money to buy equipment (such as a camera and an editing suite) and simply start working. He said, "If it were any other career, you'd need a diploma. But in film, your credentials are what you make; if you make a nice film, that's your diploma."

I said I would pray about it and look at all the options before deciding. Lisa and I scouted all the film schools in the city. All of them gave us a dark feeling. We would talk to the head of the place, and they would show us the films the students had made. Let's just say, I never want to see those films again.

It would have been one thing if they had told us that each person learns the skills and then works on their own film, but it wasn't that way. Perhaps I would have gone and studied if it had it been like that. Instead, every student has to help the others with their film, and in turn, everyone helps you. So if one student decides to make a film on

something that you don't like, you have to help them. And if I never wanted to see those student films again, I most certainly didn't want to be a part of making them. A film that lasts only ten minutes in viewing can take months to make.

So I checked abroad in Vancouver and in Los Angeles – the two major film cities of the world. It was the same story. I got accepted into the two schools I applied to: the George Lucas Film School in California and the Vancouver Film School. I went to Vancouver to check it out, as I had to speak at a convention there anyway. As soon as I walked into the building, I got the same dark feeling. As soon as I watched the student films, I knew I didn't want to see them again and much less be a part of the making of them.

Questions came to my mind, "Why? Why can't I go to film school? Why can't I decide what I want to do just like everyone else does?" All my classmates had gone to study something or other. Yet besides the darkness I felt in these places, something strong inside me told me that this was not what I was supposed to do. In my heart, I knew I was supposed to go back home, back to Colombia, back to the place that all my friends had left to discover the world and study abroad. For very personal reasons, I did not want to go back. In fact, it was the last thing I wanted to do. So for the two weeks I was in Vancouver, I argued with the Lord, "Why can't I choose what I want to do just like everyone else does?" And one day as I was walking into a household to eat dinner with some very sweet people in Vancouver, the Lord Jesus answered me.

I wasn't particularly praying in that moment. I was just entering someone's house, but he knew all the questions I had been asking in my mind that month and he spoke right to my heart and said, "I had to go through the same thing. If you follow me, it will lead to your death."

There is nothing that is as sweet as hearing his voice. Though the words he spoke to me weren't exactly what I wanted to hear, I was so happy just to hear him. He could have said anything.

"If you follow me…" If. In other words, he was saying it was my choice.

A few days later, I was on a plane to Colombia. I must have cried for most of the flight. The Lord Jesus wept the night before he knew he had to die. He didn't want to go through that either. It was so comforting to know that he knew exactly how I was feeling and that he cared. Matthew 26:39 says, "And he went a little further and fell on his face, praying and saying, O my Father, if it be possible, let this cup pass from me; nevertheless not as I will, but as thou wilt."

On the plane in the midst of my tears I prayed, "If this is your will for me, then I accept it. Just, please Lord, give me something to do, keep me busy with what you want while I am down there."

The Lord did a good job of keeping his end of the deal and keeping me busy. I worked on transcribing and translating several of my dad's sermons he had given for the Spanish radio stations into English. A commentary on the book of Daniel was the very first book to come out of this work. It quickly became a bestseller on Amazon.

Also, when I got back home from Canada, Lisa and I began writing our very first full-length feature movie script called *La Montaña*. This was a true story of some of the things that had happened to my dad and me in our adventures in the jungles and mountains of the countryside. We had tried to write it before that, and spent years doing it. But when we gave it over to my parents to read, they were quiet. They did not say a single word. That's when we knew something was off. This time, however, divine inspiration took over, and in a matter of only a few months, it was written. And there were no fights between us during the process like there had been the last time we had tried.

After we finished writing this new draft and gave it to my parents to read, they were excited. Dad and mom wanted to help us produce this film. Dad started handing out copies of the script to all his friends. That's when I knew he had liked it. He handed it to all the real characters of the story: the

guerrilla leaders, the paramilitary leaders, the generals. They all loved it. I spoke personally to Eduardo and Noel, the two main characters, after they had read it. Noel sent me a letter via his mother-in-law saying me he wanted to help in any way he could. On one of our trips to the jungle to distribute Bibles and books and install a water plant for some of the farmers caught between the war, we got to see Eduardo, a main character in the film. This was the hard-nosed guerrilla leader who at first is skeptical of dad and anything having to do with God, but at the end of the film, has a change for the better and ends up making peace with his enemies, the paramilitaries.

On that trip, I asked Eduardo twice if there was anything in the script he thought needed to be changed. Both times, he said no. I thought he wasn't really understanding my question, because naturally I thought there must be something he didn't like or was in disagreement with. The third time I asked, I made myself a little more explicit and said, "Listen, I want to tell the truth. That is all. If there is anything that you think should be changed in this script because it is not quite true and needs to be corrected, now is the time to tell me, because I can change it."

He looked me square in the eyes and said, "Why would I want to change the truth of what really happened?" That is when I knew that the Lord had helped us nail the veracity of the story.

One day in the kitchen of Lisa's apartment, we heard some terrible news. There had been a terrorist attack and lots of people had died. It was pretty normal news for us in Colombia, but it devastated us, nonetheless. My sister and I talked about it for a little while and got so sad that we knelt down in the kitchen to pray, weeping as we asked the Lord that if there were anything we could do for our country to make it better, that he would use us, even if it was with only a small grain of sand.

Then Lisa went for a month-long acting course in LA. She came back with greater faith than I had ever seen in her before. In that trip, the Lord truly showed her that he loved her and that he was not a mean God who was out to destroy her dreams, but one

who wanted to help her fulfill all the desires of her heart if she only placed him first. I was astounded at the new Lisa.

Before that trip, she and I both thought we needed a hot-shot Hollywood director to make this movie for us. The movie *Invictus* had come out, and we thought, "Man, if only Clint Eastwood would come and direct this film, we would be set!"

But when Lisa came back from California, after rubbing shoulders with other directors and seeing their sets and their little world, she told me, "There is nothing that they do there that you and I can't do just as well or better here with our friends and our people. We've got this!" The Lord had gotten a firm hold on her and that was a game changer.

The experience of making *La Montaña* was amazing, to say the least. So many times I thought, "Not even a ten-million-dollar budget could provide the lighting that the Lord has just provided for us." We would arrive at a certain place and everything would look grey and dull, and then suddenly when the cameras were out and the actors in place, the sun would shine through the clouds and make everything beautiful. And as soon as we were finished filming the scene, like clockwork, the sun would hide back behind the clouds, making everything grey and dull once again.

The Lord was in every detail, even the smallest one. Every actor was perfect for their role and they weren't hard to find. When we would do a casting, Lisa and I would just look at each other and know without a doubt that this was the perfect person for the part.

The actor for Eduardo was the spitting image of Eduardo himself, and so were all the rest of the characters. There were very few arguments with Lisa. Only one or two, to be honest, during the whole process, which took about a year and six months. And even those arguments were not really arguments at all. It was as if we were synchronized. Filming each scene was magical because I thought that nothing could be the way I had imagined it. Yet, when we finished a scene, it would turn out exactly the way I had seen it as we were writing it. Many times, Lisa would look at me,

and we would be thinking the same thing, "How is this possible!?"

Lisa's outgoing behavior was perfect when it came to conveying our ideas to our crew and cast. I was behind all the cameras making sure the picture turned out perfect. As the directors of this project, we made a good team. The postproduction turned out to be a lot more work than it was to film it, but we had so much fun editing, color-correcting, musicalizing, etc., all in the little recording studio we had dug out of the mountainside wall of my parents' apartment years before.

The cost of producing it ended up being about as much as it would have been for me to go and study film at a good university. Film schools are not cheap. Movies are not cheap to make either, but this one turned out to be a lot less expensive than most film budgets are because technology had improved to the point where good equipment was now within a reasonable price range and also because every person that worked on it (including my family) volunteered and donated their time.

The Lord had made it so that we were independent and free to work on whatever was in our hearts, not in whatever was in other people's hearts, and we had the time of our lives doing it!

La Montaña became one of the most viewed movies in Colombia, reaching seven million people on YouTube alone! Someone we don't know posted it on there, and we were very surprised at all the views. That does not count all the other people in the jungles and mountains who do not have access to the Internet.

We premiered the movie on the 20th of July in 2012 (Colombia's Independence Day), in Cubarral, Meta, the little town where we had filmed it. We installed a big theater screen and a 5.1 surround sound system.

We were expecting about 200 people. Were we ever surprised when 1,400 people showed up! We had to reschedule three more events in that same town and then all the mayors of all the surrounding towns wanted us to show it to their communities. We ended up doing a yearlong road trip all across the countryside

of Colombia in all the little towns and villages that wanted to see it.

The response of all the people, every time we would show it, amazed me. Never had I seen an audience give a movie a five-minute standing ovation. It's something that happens when you see a live production, like an opera or a play, but not a movie!

The only rejection we ever had was from the Ministry of Culture. We had wanted to show it nationwide in all the theaters, but they did not accept it as a Colombian film. When Lisa went to submit it and asked why they had not accepted it – since all the actors, the directors, the producers, and even hundreds of soldiers from the Colombian Army, were all Colombian citizens– they were very rude and said, "There is a mistake in the credits; you named the title of 'Sound Engineer' wrong."

"Okay, that's an easy one to fix." Lisa said. "We'll correct that one mistake in the credits and hand it to you again next week."

"No," they insisted, "it doesn't really matter whether or not you correct that. Just know that this is the only film in the history of movies here in Colombia that was not accepted by us."

What was meant to be an insult actually made me feel a lot better. I had seen many of the movies they had accepted, and I was glad when ours was rejected.

They only represented a handful of people in the Ministry of Culture that didn't like it and decided to ban it from being shown in all the major cities. Millions all over the countryside already loved it. Never could we have imagined how much everyone would be able to relate to the story and how it would spark such a deep longing inside of every single person, a longing for real, true, God-given peace.

The making of the movie, *La Montaña* had nothing to do with me or my sister's petty little dreams of becoming filmmakers. It was the direct result of following the Lord, even under the condition that following him would only lead to death.

I don't know if he meant a literal death, although many true followers of the Lord throughout history have had to face that. I do

know that everyone who follows him must die to their sin, to their un-forgiveness, to their own plans and anything else he may require. It is different for every person. But the thing about it, is that after death, (whether it is a literal death or merely a genuine conversion), there is also life! Only this time it is his life. "Christ in you the hope of glory," the apostle Paul wrote.[10]

* * *

Now, back to the play. Every time we would go down to the theater to rehearse, again I would get a glimpse into that dark film/theater world I had not wanted to be a part of and was happy that the Ministry of Culture had not let us be a part of. Actors and directors from other plays would practice in the other rooms.

We had a weeklong break, and Stephen and I went to a cozy little cottage in the mountains to be together. We had almost decided to go visit Pabel and Kelly out in Huila, but a friend lent us their little cabin

---

10 Colossians 1:27

near Bogotá, and we went there instead. At night, Stephen made me a fire outside and cooked a meal for us. As we were playing cards by the light of the fire and the moon, a phone call came in. It was my brother Russell Jr. with the bad news I mentioned in chapter 11.

"Hi Alethia. I'm so sorry. Pabel was found dead. He was hung on a tree with the weight of the Bibles he was carrying…" He kept talking, but I couldn't listen anymore.

I started weeping uncontrollably. "No! No!" I cried.

"I'm sorry," Russell said on the other end of the line.

The next day, we went back to Bogotá to continue working on the play. Soon December came and the day of the first presentation arrived.

Lisa made everything special. She bought vases and stands to decorate the entrance to the theater and the preliminary lobby with the loveliest flowers. She even had a beautiful welcome sign and our usual popcorn stand we had used for all our other premieres.

When I walked out of the dressing room, the fragrance of flowers filled the beautifully decorated room. The gross cigarette smell was gone. It had been replaced by the sweet aromas of roses and popcorn. Christmas lights turned the gloomy place into a bright little world. The dark feeling of the theater left for the time being, and it felt like a place that belonged to us alone.

Our friends who came to see it filled the atmosphere with something special and made it feel even more like home. There were no Christian signs or verses. No prayers said. No deep spiritual message within the play. But the Lord was there. Many times I have been to events where prayers were being rehearsed, Christian signs were everywhere, and an intended deep spiritual message was stated, but the presence of the Lord was not there.

We had two whole days of presentations, and on the last day, Kelly, now Pabel's widow, and her four-year-old son, David Israel, and her three-year-old daughter, Linda Estefanía, walked in to see our final show.

The lights dimmed and we got into our places. This presentation was for them.

During all the other presentations and most of this next one I was so focused on being my character that all the lights and the audience simply became invisible, unrecognized by me, the eighty-year-old lady.

I was now in a scene where Lisa and I listened to everyone else talk for a couple of minutes while gobbling down *chocorramos* (my grandma's favorite kind of chocolate-covered vanilla cake). Lisa did the re-enactment of my grandma's love for *chocorramos* and the way she eats them, perfectly. It was the one scene where both of us merely stood side by side, not talking, just munching while the rest talked. It was in this moment when I glanced out of the corner of my eye, only to see Kelly, David Israel, and Linda Estefania laughing hysterically. I could tell Lisa had seen it too. The world stopped for a minute, and we both watched them, taking the moment in.

For a split second, we had become Lisa and Alethia again, not Donna and Doña Antonia. All our work had paid off in a better way than we had ever imagined. Even if it was only for a minute, Kelly and her children had forgotten their pain.

My siblings: Lisa, Russell Jr., and Dylan, all acted in the play. My brothers were also actors in La Montaña. We are blessed to be a very close family.

Chapter 18
Jorge Pirata's Warning

February 18, 2015, La Picota Penitentiary, Bogotá Two months later

I WOKE UP to a normal day in the city of Bogotá. Stephen and I had our special coffee time that we enjoy every morning with breakfast before our day begins. As is usual, we talked about our day and of what each of us had to do. I had to go to the prison that morning to talk to Jorge Pirata, our family's longtime ex-paramilitary friend from the Eastern Plains of Colombia.

Jorge Pirata had desperately been trying to get in touch with Dad for the past two weeks, saying he urgently needed to talk to him in person. Dad had tried going a week before, but he had gotten to the prison ten minutes past visiting hours and they hadn't let him in.

Dad hesitated in trying to go again because not less than two months before, twenty farmers from the Sumapaz region had been

thrown in jail by the authorities, all charged with rebellion. One of them was Dad's friend Hilber. When Dad heard this had happened, he hired Mónica Rodríguez, our friend and lawyer, to try and get Hilber out of jail along with all the others.

Mónica had gone to the courthouse to retrieve the case against the twenty farmers and was instead handed a recording where there was a case against my dad and an order out for his arrest.

We still do not know if it was a friend inside the system trying to warn us of what was happening or if it was a simple act of divine providence intervening on our behalf. Whatever the case, we were warned, but not because the government *wanted* us to be warned.

Mónica called people in high ranks of authority to see if this audio was true, but they all said it had been revoked. We thought this was the case because my dad had recently travelled to a missionary convention in Canada at the end of January and had not been stopped at the airport. However, as a safety precaution, he figured it was best to be prudent and not do things that might put him under further investigation. Visiting a prison, though a completely legal action, might attract unnecessary attention for him.

Now a week later, he was sending me. I was the only other person we knew of (besides Dad, of course) who Jorge Pirata had put on the ten-person visiting list he was allowed to have. I had no clue I was on his visiting list until that morning, even though we had been there before. The previous visits were a result of a special permission the government had given us to show our film in the prison and to interview all the former paramilitary men.

Jorge Pirata and his men were some of the main characters portrayed in our movie *La Montaña,* and we had really wanted them to see it. The Lord miraculously provided the way for my two brothers and sister to show it there. To our great surprise, all of the prisoners in the paramilitary ward, including Jorge Pirata, gave the movie a standing ovation and clapped for about three minutes while the credits rolled. We had been a little

nervous as to how they would react, since it was about them, after all.

I had gone after that to interview Jorge Pirata with Dad and a reporter from the USA and another time afterward because they all wanted Albert and Dad to pray for them.

This was my first time going alone, but I felt peace. I made my way through the rings of security in the prison until I finally arrived at Jorge Pirata's cell. After waiting for twenty minutes because he had other guests to attend to that day, Jorge Pirata invited me into his little cell. I sat down to find out what his urgent message was.

"Alethia, the reason I have been trying to get a hold of your dad is because two weeks ago, I received a call from Martín Sombra, who told me to contact him urgently because in his ward, he saw four guerrilla convicts testifying against your dad to the authorities."

Martín Sombra was an ex-guerrilla commander who had been captured in 2008, several months before the three Americans and twelve Colombians who were being held hostage by the FARC were miraculously rescued by the Colombian Army.

Sombra had had some sort of a personal change for the better in prison, and as soon as he found out that there were guerrillas testifying falsely against my father, he called Jorge Pirata, a former paramilitary commander. Ironically, and perhaps providentially, two former enemies joined together in an effort to help save their missionary from prison.

Don Jorge continued, "Look, I want you to know that I am your dad's friend and that my men and I are willing to testify in favor of him. I am a witness to all the missionary work he did in the areas where I commanded. Whenever we would stop him in roadblocks, the only thing he would do was share the love of God with us and give us Bibles and water. I still have the Bible he gave me, along with all the other books."

Soldiers, guerrillas, paramilitaries and country folk would all stop Dad along the road to receive books, radios and the Bible.

He pointed to his little bookshelf above his bed and there was the Bible my dad had given him, some ten years before, along with the other Christian literature.

He continued, "I still have these books. They are my treasures. Tell your dad he can count on me. I had to do everything possible to warn him because I am incapable of letting my friend go to prison without doing everything in my ability to stop it. You know Alethia, it is very easy to be put into prison, and very hard to get back out again."

I thanked him from the bottom of my heart and told him I would give the message to my dad. Relieved that I had accomplished my mission and was now free to leave, I got up to say good-bye, but Jorge stopped me, "You can't leave yet. See, they lock the prison doors when visitors come in on Wednesdays, and they don't open them again until 2:00 p.m."

"Great," I thought. It was only 11:00 a.m., and I was stuck in there for another three hours. Prisons made me a little claustrophobic.

But Jorge was very kind to me, and so were all his friends. It wasn't that bad. He invited me to eat lunch with him and other former paramilitary leaders at 12 o'clock.

Afterward, Jaime, another leader and also a friend of my father's, gave me an hour-long harp recital. It was beautiful. One song he wrote was called, "The Sad Ballad of the Prisoner." He walked me through the prison and showed me all the landscapes he had painted onto the boring grey walls. They were lovely. I wrote down all the names of

the songs he played to put them on the radio stations and before I knew it, it was 2:00 and I was free to leave.

Dad was in the living room talking to an American journalist when I arrived from the prison. When I finished telling him the messages from Martín Sombra and Jorge Pirata, his face turned white and he called his lawyer, Mónica. Ten minutes later, Mónica arrived and we told her what had happened.

Mónica is a fragile, single lady in her fifties. God has cured her of cancer and of various other diseases. He was most likely preparing her for this very day. I no sooner finished telling Mónica what was happening when another phone call came in.

It was my grandma Pat calling from the northern coast of Colombia. B-pa had just fallen and broken his leg that very morning. They were in the hospital awaiting a surgery. She passed the phone to him and all he could manage to say to me in the weakest voice ever was, "Help… I want to see Russell. I want to see my son…"

Then Grandma came on the phone again, "He really wants to see your dad. It's the only thing he ever says. You guys have to come."

"Dad, we have to go to Santa Marta. B-pa is not doing well, and he wants to see you," I said.

Right then, Dad received a call from a captain of the army in Sumapaz telling him to go and present himself to a police headquarters downtown, "just to answer some basic questions and explain yourself," he said casually. The captain gave him the number of the policeman who was waiting for him, and my dad gave the policeman a call.

When Dad hung up, I asked him who it was, and he said, "It's some policeman who knows about the case against me and wants me to go over and meet up with him."

"Did he sound nice?" I asked.

"No," my dad answered, "he sounded upset. It looks like I need to go over and make friends with him. Clear the situation up a little."

"But what about B-pa? You need to go to Santa Marta," I told him.

"Yes, and I will, but first I need to clear this thing up. We already have tickets to visit B-pa the first week of March. By then, this will all be resolved. I also have that trip with the Boyds next week. Don't worry sweetie; it will all work out."

Dad, Stephen, and I had bought tickets beforehand for March, at B-pa's request, a few months back. We had gone to visit him and had promised to go again. He and Stephen met for the first and only time and talked for about two hours. B-pa had really liked him.

The Boyds were friends of my parents from Indiana who had invited Mom and Dad on a trip to Machu Picchu (all expenses paid) at the end of the month.

"Dad, at least wait until Hugo Tovar, the other lawyer, gets here. He might have another opinion of what you should do."

But it was of no use; Dad had his mind set. He stormed out the door with Mónica and the American journalist following behind. There was nothing I could do to stop him. My kind-hearted, trusting, and somewhat naïve dad had rushed out to make friends with the police officer who had called – someone who would later prove to be one of his main accusers.

Meanwhile, I went up to my room to cry. I knew in my heart it was going to be the end for B-pa. His body would not be able to handle this. I knelt down and said a prayer for him. Then I remembered how I had gotten through Lucy's death. As I prayed, I imagined how happy he would soon be, playing and running with his dog Toby. Toby was B-pa's dog back when he was eighteen. B-pa could never talk about Toby without his eyes tearing up. I knew he would be happy. My sadness went away.

Hugo Tovar Marroquín, the lawyer who had helped get my Jewish friend, Ernesto, out of prison, arrived about thirty minutes after my dad had left, and I showed him everything, even the recording we had gotten previously saying that my dad was being investigated and that the phone had been tapped. The police hadn't found any evidence in the conversations, so the investigation of the phone line was dropped; however, we

didn't know if they were still after him. Hugo was thoughtful and said that I needed to gather all the evidence I could. He told me I was to go back to the jail and get Jorge Pirata and the other paramilitaries and anyone else I knew of to give declarations immediately.

As soon as he left, my mom received a phone call from Sammy, who had received a phone call from Jean Bergeron, our representative in Canada; the whole thing had been a trap and my dad was in jail. The police only gave Dad one phone call, so he called Jean Bergeron, our friend with all the contacts, so that she could get everyone to pray.

The gravity of the situation had hit me: my dad was in prison, and who knew when we would get him out again? It might take years because in Colombia there is no such thing as bail — where you can pay the government money in return for being let out of prison as proof that you will attend all the hearings until your final verdict. These processes can take years, and here those years are many times spent in jail.

Life as I knew it was quickly falling apart. I was already feeling claustrophobic for my dad at the mere thought of four walls surrounding him for years on end. Ever since I saw the movie *The Hurricane*, where the boxing champion gets imprisoned unjustly for his whole life, I have believed prison is a fate worse than death.

However, men such as Richard Wurmbrand had survived prison and torture. He had made it out alive after fourteen years in a communist prison in Romania, and there had been a purpose behind it all. (More of Richard Wurmbrand's story is in chapter 20.) "The bride was in the arms of the bridegroom," Wurmbrand preached with conviction. "We were with God. We didn't know that we were in prison. So Communists persecute those who believe in Christ. Christians are happy to suffer! But it is your job to help stop these sufferings."

The only reason why I knew this particular message by heart was because we had made a documentary about him, and that was one of the quotes we had used. In editing, you have to see things over and over again, and it had stuck. I had also read his book *In God's Underground* and it was truly amazing how the Lord was with him and used him so much during those fourteen long years of torture, lack of sun, and even in the three years of complete solitary underground confinement. God had been with him through it all.

When I read Wurmbrand book, I realized that I would rather be with God in prison, even in the most horrible conditions, than without him in paradise. Those stories were horrible, yet also amazing.

* * *

Different people react in different ways. I remember when I was on a soccer team, and we were playing in the semi-final of a championship out in the Eastern Plains of the country. This specific area we were in had seen a lot of war, and as a result, the people in that area were more prone to distrust outsiders. A men's competition had already been held, and the fight between the team from the city of Bogotá and one called Puerto Rico, one of the most war-trodden towns, got so heated in one game that one of the players from the little town took a gun out and started threatening the other team.

Soon soldiers came and surrounded the field, and the game continued under the surveillance of the army. The guys had already had several competitions, and I felt left out. So I announced a contest on one of our radio stations. I said, "I am the captain of a team from Bogotá, and we will be having a New Year's championship with any and all girls' teams that would like to come and compete."

To be honest, I didn't have a team when I announced the event. I immediately went to Bogotá and called any girls I could think of, including Lisa, to join me in making up this new team. These girls had never played before, but we had a good trainer: my friend Juan Miguel, Sammy's younger brother, who was a professional in that department.

Seven teams from all over the countryside showed up, and the little school of the community lent us their facilities to lodge them during the event. My team made it to the semi-finals, somehow.

When we began the semi-final, it was obvious from the way we played that I had just made up a team a few months before and named myself the captain. For these other girls, this was their life. They handled the ball so well that they danced circles around us. I was lost on the field for the first half of the game (causing my whole team to be lost as well), until one of those big girls decided to trip me on purpose. These relentless country girls made it clear they were showing us city slickers who was boss. It didn't help that we also looked the part, most of us being blonde, lighter skinned, and thinner.

"Rip their legs! Show 'em who's tougher!" Their coach yelled on the side.

I got so angry I forgot myself. The referee called a foul, I got up from my injury, and suddenly what had been the impenetrable fortress of tough soccer girls barring our way past mid-field during the whole first half of the game became my territory. I made it singlehandedly all the way to the other side of the field, dodging all the tough girls who were in my way. Never had I been able to do that during the game until the moment I got mad enough.

Although not a good quality to have all the time, the feeling of losing yourself in an emotion such as anger can sometimes help you be more determined and braver than you would have been without it. It sort of gives you that extra amount of audacity you wouldn't have had otherwise. We did not win that day, but we definitely gave them a good fight. After the game, I overheard one of the girls from the other team say in reference to me, "Boy, once she puts her mind to it, that girl can really play!"

* * *

Now that my dad was imprisoned, I was furious. I knew they had scored a goal on us. Enemies wanted to bring my dad down, and they were succeeding. That fury helped me, even energized me, to fight for him.

I stormed up to my room, slammed the door, and started making phone calls.

It obviously was not the right time to say it, but Stephen came and told me I needed to calm down. We had only been married

for six or seven months (depending on which wedding you were counting from) so in his defense, he was still learning about women. Had he been more experienced, he would have known that you never, ever tell a girl to calm down when she is mad. Ever. But, I did calm down after a while and took his advice: yes we did need to fight, but it was important to know *how* to fight, because it was in the *how* that we would win.

Chapter 19
John Bunyan

MY WHOLE FAMILY and I went to the police station to visit Dad, except for Stephen, who stayed to make sure we didn't miss any phone calls or visitors. They were going to transfer Dad to a real prison out in the town of Fusa, but someone called (we don't know who) and told the cops to let him spend the night at the police station instead. Mónica was crying. She blamed herself for letting him waltz into the police station like that and was a wreck when they arrested him.

We met with the policeman whom my dad had talked to previously on the phone. With a smirk on his face, he said, "Usually with cases like this, we put people in the dungeon, but we're going make an exception and let him sleep here for the night." Then we asked if we could see our dad, and he said, "It's really not allowed, but I guess we can make yet *another* exception."

Nothing bothered me more than this cop's attitude. He was pretending to play "the good

Samaritan" with an innocent man. I felt like telling him off and saying, "Quit acting like you're doing my father some sort of charity! He's innocent! He shouldn't even be here!" But I kept my wits and was as nice and polite as I could be.

"You are so kind, sir; thank you for letting us visit him," I said.

The superficial politeness between the two of us would not last very long. We went in, up the stairs, through dark halls, and finally got to my dad who was sitting in a police office. We all hugged him. My sister said, "It's nice to see you, John Bunyan!" John Bunyan was a Christian author known for finishing one of history's most beloved works of art called *The Pilgrim's Progress* while in prison. Dad was calm and peaceful.

"Well, all these years, I've only done what my conscience has told me to do, and no one can ever force anyone to go against their conscience if they are willing to risk their freedom or even their life. Now we will find out who our real friends are." He said this last part with a smile.

The time was short, so we had to say goodbye. Sammy asked the officer if he could take a video of dad. The officer said yes, and then suddenly changed his mind. Since he hadn't said anything to me about it, I had about a thirty-second window in which the officer was checking papers in another office, and I quickly got my phone on and had Dad record a brief message to everyone abroad.

"Somebody set a trap for me, and we walked into it," he stated. "There was a secret order out for my arrest, and here I am. There will be a court hearing in the morning. They are accusing me of rebellion for the missionary trips and the visits that I made into rebel territory distributing Bibles and Galcom radios."

I had just finished recording when the officer came in frantically from the other room.

"What are you doing?! Is that a video?" he asked.

"Yes, it is."

"You have to erase it."

"Okay, perhaps when I get home." I answered calmly as I walked out of the office.

186

"No, come over here and erase that video in front of me," he ordered.

This is when I realized how important the video was.

"No, I'm not going to." I said. And playing the "suffering daughter" card, I told him, "It's the only memory I have left of my father, and I'm not going to let *you* erase it."

I tried to walk out of the police station as fast as I could. But this officer made a call to his superior and would not let us leave. He even threatened my family by saying he was going to have me arrested. My brother Dylan whispered in my ear, "Quick, send it to someone fast!"

I tried sending it, but the file was too large. I quickly snuck the phone into my friend Alex's pocket, just in case they tried to take my cell phone away from me. When my family asked the officer why he was so upset about a video, he said, "I can have you all arrested too, if that's what you want!"

It is a good thing that our friend, Luisa Fernanda Avila – a major from the army and Alex's wife – was there in her army uniform. She told him he would be in so much trouble if he arrested me, then she called up her superior, and the police officer let us go.

Chapter 20

No Time for Debate

THE PROSECUTOR had been working on the case against my father for two years, since 2013, and now we only had one night (and it was already about 10:00 p.m.) to build his defense. But years of watching my parents face difficult situations straight on must have prepared us in some way. About twenty of our closest friends and family united at our house, along with Mónica and her investigator, Juan Angarita.

There was a big debate as to what we should do. A few people were saying that we needed to maintain the secrecy of our work; others were saying we needed to make it all as public as possible. I didn't understand how we could defend ourselves by keeping what we did a secret. To me, all the cards had to be laid out on the table if we wanted to win the case. But a few others said that it was dangerous and unwise for us to do that, as our work involved very sensitive things that no one knew about. We could get serious enemies as a result.

Sammy and his dad, Aníbal Hernández, felt the same way as I did. Everyone was arguing, and it was hard to make any sense of it all. We had to come up with a decision and fast. There was no time for arguments. Sammy interrupted everyone by speaking above the noise, "We need to bring it all into the light, no matter what the consequences are!" Everyone stopped talking and listened. "It was the last thing that my father-in-law said to us before we left the police station, and I agree with him. This is not the time to hide anything we do; this is the time for us to expose it."

"I agree completely," I said.

My mom, Aníbal, Marthica, Dylan, and Lisa voiced their agreement as well.

"Dad, please pray for the Lord to guide us and show us to how to defend Russell in the best way possible," Sammy said. We all bowed our heads as Aníbal prayed.

In an instant, adrenaline filled our bodies and everyone, including my youngest brother Dylan, age fifteen, got to work immediately.

I posted the video – the one the policeman had wanted me to erase – on YouTube and on our *La Montaña* Facebook page. After only a few hours, thousands of people had already seen it and were tweeting and posting on Facebook about it. Soon many of the main news networks, such as the *Miami Herald,* CNN, CBN, *El Tiempo,* and others had posted the video on their web pages and were using what Dad had said in it to make a story. People everywhere were praying for his release. It is a good thing that I had kept a record with my camera of all the trips we had done to war zones. I had a lot of evidence that proved my dad was passing out Bibles and other books to all sides of the war. I made a folder of everything.

Juan interviewed everyone there, except for the immediate family. Dylan and my cousin Kaleb had to transcribe all the witnesses' interviews. Our friends and co-workers – Fercho, Alex, and others – got busy collecting all the interviews and reports there had been in the past about my dad and the ministry. Sammy made phone calls to contact Voice of the Martyrs (VOM) Canada, VOM Finland, Spirit of Martyrdom, Galcom, and other respected organizations to ask them to write letters confirming the fact that my dad was a missionary and not a terrorist. Everyone wrote amazing letters and responded immediately.

* * *

The Voice of the Martyrs (VOM) is a worldwide organization that was founded by Richard Wurmbrand after he was released from his fourteen years of imprisonment when the communist regime took over Romania, his country. During his time in prison and afterward, he wrote amazing books such as *Jesus a Friend for Terrorists, Christ on the Jewish Road, An Answer to the Atheists in Moscow,* and others that expose communism for what it really is – but expose it with love.

However, love goes hand in hand with truth, and these books were the cause of several kidnappings, including the time when the guerrillas kidnapped my father and

me. My dad had handed out close to seven thousand of Richard Wurmbrand's books, risking his life and the lives of all his workers in guerrilla territory.

I happened to be on the "wrong" trip, meaning I was not on the trip in which these books were handed out, but instead on the trip in which the guerrilla leaders had already read them and were furious. Wurmbrand's *Marx and Satan* book is one of a kind. In one reading, it unveils who Marx really was by using his own writings in a way no other book does. I honestly believe it should be required reading for all students.

* * *

Marx and Satan and other books were gathered and compiled by our team as evidence in my dad's defense.

My other little brother, Russell Jr. (age twenty-two) was in the United States at the time studying for his pilot's license. His studies happened to be in the same town where VOM USA had their headquarters. Russell Jr. tried to get the leaders of this organization to help my dad, but for some reason, they had other priorities that night. Had Richard Wurmbrand still been alive, the response would have been completely different. Yet God still set up angels to help us in our darkest hours. Angela Lipscomb Thompson was one of them; I met her years before during a VOM conference in Alabama and still had her contact. She was not one of the big leaders. She was just a small representative of the many hundreds they have, but she sent us everything we needed: the VOM magazines with all the pictures and stories about us. She could not believe this was happening and did everything she could to help our case.

We worked all night. If I slept an hour, that is a generous estimate. Up until now, the work that God had my family doing in this country had remained a secret. Only a few of our closest friends knew what we really did. That was changing by the minute. The time had come for our work to be exposed and brought to the light.

Dad speaking to our Páez friends.

Chapter 21
Dad's Speech

THE NEXT MORNING, we headed out as soon as we could to see what time they had scheduled the hearing. Our close friends and family were already waiting for us when we arrived. There was still no news of the hearing, so we went back home to continue working on his defense and keep spreading the news.

Friends everywhere were sending in reports, signed and authorized, stating that Russell Martín Stendal was their close friend and that they witnessed to the fact that he was a missionary. I printed these out and went back to the courthouse, but there was still no news.

Then I went with Juan, the investigator, to interview Colonel Yunda, an officer in the military who had worked closely with my dad in Cauca. I felt as if angels filled the room as he was talking. He spoke of all the books and Bibles and how whole areas had changed as a

result. He said that was why the military liked to work with my dad.

Dad was right. In one day, we realized who our true friends were and which friends were only there in the good times. There were "friends" of my dad who didn't have time for an interview. And there were others who simply did not speak up. But our real friends stood up for him in a time when he needed it the most.

As soon as we finished the interview with Colonel Yunda, we went back to the courthouse, only to find my mom looking very weakened and frail. "RCN just put out a horrible news clip about your dad," she whispered to me. That day her voice was almost inaudible due to a recent throat infection.

On two of Colombia's main news channels (similar to CNN or FOX in the USA) was a video of my dad, with his hands cuffed, in the middle of two policemen; the headline was "Alias, 'The Gringo,' of the FARC Captured for Rebellion."

Right after my mom saw the news clip, she went over to the officer who had arrested my dad the night before and had threatened to arrest me, and she asked him why they would allow the reporters to film such a terrible, untrue story. The policeman's snarky reply was, "That is your daughter's fault."

When our good friend Major Luisa Avila overheard this, she confronted him and said, "So, you get furious at Martín's daughter for filming a video and told her that it's because you wanted to 'protect' him, but then you let all the reporters film him and get another police officer to state in front of live news that Martín is the guerrilla leader, alias, 'El Gringo?' Where is your big need and concern to protect Martín? Why, if you were trying to 'protect' him from 'exposure,' did you let the police give the press a false declaration?"

My dad told me afterward that the officer found out about the video I posted online at about 2:00 p.m. and then started being really nasty after that. The colonel of the police that Dad was with then made a phone call to the prosecutor, and my dad heard him say, "We

need to sink him NOW! Before the hearing starts!"

The false news reports came out at about 2:30 p.m. When I talked to a reporter from a news channel about what had happened, he said, "RCN just runs on anything the police and the district attorney's office tell them, and they don't verify to see if it's true."

RCN and Caracol are the main channels here, and they are the ones that feed the news to the entire international news department. Soon this whole, "Alias, 'the Gringo,' of the FARC" thing was put into international media. It only makes me wonder how many other people's names and reputations they have ruined, or tried to ruin, just because someone stood up to them.

That was a low point in the day. It was as if the jury had already decided to put my dad in prison for fifteen years. The thought of having to go through a hearing soon seemed like a waste of time. It was evident they had already made up their minds about him. My poor mom was going through an awful time seeing her husband shamed like that on news channels that she faithfully watched every night.

Lisa took good care of her during this time. I was trying really hard not to cry in public, but the tears were welling up inside me like a fountain. I couldn't talk to anyone. But Stephen knows me well. He knelt down to the level where I was seated, and as he stroked my face and looked at me in the eyes, he said, "This is going to be happening a lot more. We can't let it get to us."

Somehow, I managed to contain my grief, and so did all of my family. We were devastated inside, but none of us would show it, or maybe we didn't know how.

Suddenly, a man who had been a tough former paramilitary and years ago had surrendered came running into the building completely shattered and weeping. At the top of his lungs he wailed, "How could they do this to Martín? It's so unfair! I should be the one in prison!"

My family, who already had enough emotions to deal with that day, comforted him as he cried.

* * *

Meanwhile, in La Vega, my *abuelita* Cecilia
(my cute little grandma that had approved
of Stephen) was being taken care of by my
aunts who cater to her every need and are very
careful not to create any stress, scared that it
may affect her health. They had heard that
dad had been put in prison and were wanting
to talk about it in private without Abuelita
being present. They thought that this news
would not be good for her and took every
precaution possible to not let her find out. So
they turned the TV to the Caracol channel for
her to watch and left her in the living room
by herself, while they discussed the situation.
A yell from my grandmother came from
the TV room, "Ay no! Dios mío! Volvieron a
secuestrar a mi chinito!" Basically meaning,
"Oh no, they kidnapped my boy again!"

She had misunderstood the report and
thought the FARC had kidnapped him again.
So much for my aunts trying to keep it a
secret from her!

* * *

More than the press releasing an untrue story about my dad and ruining his reputation (although that was pretty bad) was the foreboding sensation that we had already lost the case. That is what those news reports did to us.

I had never truly believed anything the news said, thinking there were way too many interests in between them and the truth to make for a clean story. Besides, I had always seen police officers making all these declarations about what had "really happened" and I always wondered, "Am I supposed to believe the word of a man I do not know? Where is the evidence? Why don't they ever show any sort of evidence?"

Sure enough, here they had done the same thing with my dad. An image of him with handcuffs on, in between two cops, a big headline saying whatever they wanted it to say, a stranger stating the headline as if it were a fact, and again, no evidence. But most people do trust them. The problem with this was that we had become a target. My dad's life, along with all his family's life,

was in danger because the FARC have lots of enemies, and we were now highlighted worldwide as being part of them.

The hearing was finally scheduled for 3:30 p.m., and about eighty of my dad's closest friends and family were there. Four other lawyers who sympathized with dad's work, including Hugo Tovar, were also there giving Mónica advice. When my husband and I saw a huddle of five lawyers all counseling together, Stephen whispered in my ear, "It looks like the defense team for some mafia guy; there are so many lawyers working on this case!"

I walked up the stairs to our designated courtroom and saw dozens of reporters and cameras and lights. At first, I thought they were there for a different case, but then I realized that ours was the big story they were telling. Lisa and Sammy did a wonderful job on the interviews they gave. In one interview my sister told the reporters, "The witnesses testifying against my dad are convicts, people who have proven to be a danger to society. But we have witnesses that are respectable citizens of society. We will see which ones are more credible."

My mom went to the bathroom right before the hearing and found Mónica in tears. When she asked her what was wrong, Mónica said, "I pray that I might win this case to make up for so many other cases I've worked on that were worthless."

Before the trial, we asked dad who he wanted to defend him out of all the lawyers present. Without hesitation he said Mónica. Frail and timid Mónica, whose hands were shaking and eyes were teary. Mónica, who went to the bathroom first to pray and beg God to help her. Anyone else would have probably chosen to go with one of the big guys: Hugo Tovar, Javier Vargas, or Ever Castro – confident looking men in nice suits, seemingly unhindered by the circumstances, who appeared resolute and unwavering. But my dad has a knack for seeing things in people that others don't, and he saw something in Mónica. He wouldn't have it any other way.

Perhaps he realized that the strength of our good Lord is found more perfectly in the weak. The weak are those who have been so broken for God that they no longer rely on their own strength, but on his. This sort of weakness has nothing to do with race, gender, or age.

> *And he said unto me, My grace is sufficient for thee; for my strength is made perfect in weakness.*
> (2 Corinthians 12:9)

We came into the courtroom feeling as if my dad had already been declared guilty. It felt hopeless.

I am naturally a very claustrophobic person, only because I had once been stuck in an elevator far too long with about ten other girls crowding me. There were too many of us for the little amount of oxygen we had to share.

My dad is also claustrophobic because for five months he was tied to a tree with a nylon rope. The dense leaves of the tall trees deep in the Colombian jungle blocked any sunlight, and he was only allowed to move when it was time to go to the bathroom. The thought of him being trapped within walls for ten or fifteen years was overwhelming for me. One time we both were in the elevator when just as the doors were closing, we both decided to jump out! That's when I realized that we were the same in that sense but for different reasons.

As we sat down in the first row facing the hearing, I whispered in my sister's ear, "This is like in *The Voyage of the Dawn Treader* when Lucy, Caspian, and Edmund all get sold as slaves. It only lasted for a day in the book, you know."[11]

Everyone waited for the judge to come in as the press took pictures. Policemen escorted my dad into the area. Dad's eyes scouted the room as if he were searching for someone, when finally his eyes met mine, and once he saw me, he nodded his head as if in reassurance. I was sitting on the left side of the room with my camera in hand. I thought that perhaps the reason he was looking for

11 The Voyage of the Dawn Treader by C. S. Lewis, published by Geoffrey Bles in 1952, is the third published of seven novels in The Chronicles of Narnia (1950–1956).

me was because he wanted me to film the whole thing with my camera, and when he saw that I was ready to do precisely that, he was reassured. In all our trips together out to war zones, I had always filmed everything and took lots of pictures. He had never asked me to do it, but I always knew he was happy when I did.

The police officer that had given us all the trouble sat next to the prosecutor who had stacks and stacks of hundreds of papers, all "proof" against my dad. Mónica and Javier Vargas, another great lawyer and a good friend of the family, sat at another desk next to the prosecutor. Their main defense was a huge stack of the Bibles and books that Dad and others had either written or distributed.

Then, at a desk adjacent to them was my dad with Juan, the official investigator of the defense, along with the translator. There had to be a translator because there were so many documents and articles written in English that had to be translated to the judge.

My dad looked directly at the prosecutor and then the policeman and gave them a thumbs-up sign and a smile. The policeman returned the smile. I nudged my husband, "Just leave it to my dad to make friends with these guys." The prosecutor returned no smile and continued looking through all the paperwork.

The judge, a woman I guessed to be in her forties, had black curly hair and a stern, austere look on her face when she walked in and sat down.

I thought, "Great, this lady looks as if she's going to lock him up forever."

The first person that had the chance to speak was the prosecutor. He read all the witness accounts against my dad in the most monotonous dreary voice ever. They were the accounts of the four guerrillas that Jorge Pirata had told me about in our prison meeting. On and on they went telling big tales of "the gringo" going up to their camps, receiving huge sums of money. "We don't know the exact amount, but we figure it was hundreds of thousands of dollars," they said. This "gringo" worked hand in hand with both the guerrillas and the paramilitaries and knew

all the routes for the drug trade, they claimed. He was the great conspirator and leader of all these travesties. "Both the guerrillas and the paramilitaries answered only to him," the statements read.

It was so absurd; I could hardly contain my laughter. I expected their strategy would be to stretch the truth as much as they could to get their way, but these were no longer in the category of stretched truth. They were outright lies. What Dad always says was true: the enemy always overplays his hand.

Later on in an interview with the press, they asked Dad about the account of these false witnesses and he smiled and said, "The guerrillas don't just hand out thousands of dollars like that. Our experience in this country is that they take it and demand it from others."

This lasted for about an hour and a half. Then Juan, the investigator, leaned over and whispered in my dad's ear, "Now you have the right to ask the prosecutor one question." My dad raised his hand and the judge recognized him and let him ask his question. "Mr.

prosecutor, sir, with all due respect, please tell this court, out of the five or six hundred pages of documents you have been waving around that you claim make up the case against me, how many of those sheets of paper actually have my name on them?"

A stunned look came over the prosecutor's face as he leafed through his reams of documents. The judge pressed him and sternly told him that he needed to answer the question. Finally, as his face turned color, the prosecutor answered, "Eleven pages total."

At this, an exasperated sigh came from everyone in the room. Then the judge gave us a fifteen-minute break that Mónica requested.

During this break, all of my dad's lawyers made a big huddle as American football players do in their timeouts. Dad and I were intent listening to their advice. "Will I get the chance to defend myself?" Dad asked.

Unanimously, they said no. "It's not wise to defend yourself at this point." Mónica replied.

"So I can't even tell my side of the story?" Dad asked.

Mónica, Javier Vargas, Ever Castro, and Hugo Tovar talked about it for a second. "If you do talk, just say you are a family man and keep it as brief as possible," Mónica responded. Then they continued talking in their lawyer terminology, which lost me. Suddenly they came to a different conclusion. Turning to dad and me, Mónica translated their new decision to us in normal Spanish: "In fact, let's just wait for the next hearing for you to tell your side. Right now, it's best if you don't speak at all."

My dad shrugged his shoulders as if in disagreement, but he wasn't going to start an argument with them. I took pity on him because I knew what it was like to want to do something without having the approval of others. Sometimes you need that strong person backing you, enabling you to do it.

It happened countless times when Lisa and I were filming *La Montaña*. Crew members would say that one of our ideas was not possible or should not be done because of such-and-such a reason. Had it not been for Lisa, perhaps I would have also shrugged my shoulders and gone with their advice. But Lisa backed me up whole-heartedly and did not let anyone get in the way of my ideas. And I did the same for her. We had each other's backs. And as a result, the movie was made exactly the way we wanted it to be. I knew this was what I had to do for Dad right now; I needed to back him when others were telling him something different.

I said, "Look, one of my dad's best attributes is always saying the right thing at the right time. I think the best thing you could do is let him speak."

"Okay," Mónica consented. She added, "but he needs to make it as brief as possible."

One of the witnesses had accused my dad of setting up "guerrilla" radio stations. So I showed the lawyers an excerpt of our book *The Hidden Agenda*,[12] where General Barrero, the former commander of all of Colombia's Armed Forces said, in reference to our

---

12 Russell M. Stendal and Alethia Stendal, The Hidden Agenda: An Extraordinary True Story Behind Colombia's Peace Negotiations with the FARC (Ransom Press International).

ministry's radio stations, "What is the purpose of these radio stations? It is so those who are good can continue being good. And so those who are bad can change as a result of the messages they hear."

Then I showed them the video to back it up where Barrero was addressing all of his officers in a speech that ended with the words, "So if you see Martín setting up radio stations, don't take him down!"

This was proof that they weren't guerrilla radio stations but were instead backed by clean generals in the army who wanted to see a positive change in their country.

At the end of the recess, I heard Dad speak to Mom before he went back to his seat for the rest of the hearing. He looked at her and said, "No matter what happens today, you are going to Machu Picchu next week with the Boyds!"

When we all returned to our seats in the courtroom, the prosecutor read all the false witnesses' accounts *again*, in the same dull voice. I don't understand very much about trials, but I didn't know why we had to hear that all twice.

These accounts continued for hours, and something that was interesting is that none of these witnesses had any exact details. Here I am writing the account of my father's arrest, and I can give details: I can give the dates, the words that were spoken, who was with us, whether or not they were nervous. I have pictures, videos, and recordings to back it all up. These witnesses had nothing but vague tales of the "gringo" visiting their camps and "taking all this money." They said nothing of who was with him, whether or not he was alone, what exact date he went to the guerrilla camp, or exactly what commander was there on a specific trip.

Did the witnesses have records of Martín dumping huge amounts of dollars into a bank? Or suddenly becoming rich?" They had nothing. In all the years I had witnessed, never did I see my father make a trip into a war zone alone. He always had someone with him, whether it was me, or one of his "cowboys," or co-workers, or a person from

the USA or Canada who wanted to know about his missionary work in the countryside. The witnesses described none of this. People such as Len Carter, Allan McGuirl, Jon Dufendach, Javier Vargas, my mom, my brothers, Lisa, Sammy, Deanne Landers, Albert Luepnitz, Allan Isaacs, Jean Bergeron, and Sandy Bergeron have accompanied him on his trips to war zones.

We are all witnesses of the fact that my dad has only been, and will only ever be, a missionary to everyone he encounters along the way.

Finally, the prosecutor was done, and it was our investigator's turn to speak. He began to recount the story of my dad's life and his mission work, but was cut off abruptly by the judge, who said to Mónica, "He is taking too long. He is not a witness!"

This happened about three times, and finally Mónica told him to simply read all the witness accounts on our side. For me, two witnesses were extremely important. One was Marta's account; she was an honest social worker for the prisons. She said that one of my fathers accusers, Alexander Ramirez (not to be confused with our friend and co-worker Alex Ramirez,) had sent her to tell my dad that if he didn't pay this inmate seventy thousand dollars, he would falsely testify against Dad in court. This was blatant proof of extortion and completely discredited the false witnesses. My dad never paid him a cent.

The other key witness on our case was Major Luisa Perdomo Avila. She talked about the army and how many generals had all backed up his missionary endeavors, including the former commander of Colombia's entire armed forces, General Barrero. Then they read the excerpt I had shown them previously of the general's words in our book *The Hidden Agenda.*

After this, Mónica requested that my dad be given the chance to speak about his missionary endeavors in all the war-afflicted regions. So far, it seemed as if this judge was much more lenient toward the prosecutor's side. She had just given him three hours to talk with absolutely no interruptions. He even got to say the whole thing twice! And now

she kept on abruptly and fiercely interrupting Mónica and our investigator, Juan, and they hadn't even been speaking for more than a few minutes. I thought for sure this judge was going to lock Dad up forever.

The judge responded to Mónica's question in the same hard-nosed manner she had used toward our side of the debate for the past three hours. "Yes," she answered sharply, "but I am going to please *beg* that his intervention be *brief* and above all *pertinent!* I am not going to stand for any sort of speeches or exhortations of absolutely anything! The only information he can say will be related to the elements of proof and to what the prosecutor has used and discovered for this hearing."

"How unfair," I thought. "Now the defense has to be brief? Why don't we get three uninterrupted hours as well?"

But Dad didn't seem phased by it.

"Thank you so much Your Honor," he calmly replied. "My parents brought me here when I was eight years old in 1964 and raised me in Colombia. I was kidnapped in 1983 by the 7th Front of the FARC. In that kidnapping I met the guerrilla Noel Pérez. He was one of the captors who got nearer to God and had a change in heart. Noel spoke well of me and Manuel Marulanda came and let me go, telling me that I could continue my missionary work in their areas. They released me on January 3, of 1984. It was through this experience that I discovered that the best way to reach my captors was with literature, Bibles, and radio stations.

"Now if we fast forward a few years to the future when the three Americans were kidnapped along with other people, generals from the Colombian Army and elements of the US government contacted me to see if I could do something to help through my contact with Noel Pérez.

"Before going into these areas, I would meet up with army intelligence officers, and then I would see them again on my return. I asked these officers to put roadblocks along the way in order to search my car going in and out of these places so as to not have to face the kind of allegations we are up against today. In various occasions, I came in contact with sick people, and every person I helped was with the

permission from the intelligence officers. I did absolutely nothing without permission."

He went on to name the intelligence generals that had worked with him during these years, giving their names and the dates of when they were in command. But then all these generals had been transferred to other parts of the country, and a new colonel came in who did not know who Dad was, and not understanding what was happening, he was the one who launched an attack.

"These officers can give you the perfect explanation of everything that happened and what the results were," he stated. "This process was hidden, and we didn't know where it was. We thought things were okay, but they weren't okay. We tried to investigate what was happening, but no one would give us an answer. When I told General Juan Pablo Amaya, who now commands in the Southeast, what was going on, he said, "Martín, a terrible mistake has been made. This shouldn't have happened."

"Juan Pablo Amaya is now in the military hospital because they operated on his hips. Or else he would be here.

"General Barrero, the former commander of the army, and General Navas lent us the military training center in Cubarral, Meta, for three months to film the movie, *La Montaña.* It would be important Your Honor, that you and the prosecutor see that movie. We have a copy we can give, and there you can see where my heart is.

"The thought that I was uniting guerrillas and paramilitaries to commit crimes is absurd. It never happened. And there are also a lot of entanglements with people that never saw me personally. I do not know this man Carrillo. I have never seen him, and as far as I know, he has never seen me. I have seen Noel Pérez on many occasions, but he is a person that has a good heart, and he ended up being key in the peace process that is now taking place.

"And to close, Libardo was one of the sick people that we helped. He returned, but then they tried to send him back to us with Carrillo with the purpose of committing crimes under our guise. But God intervened and as Carrillo was leaving their camp in the Macarena, where I suppose the Mono Jojoy was (and

I do not know the Mono Jojoy[13] either), he stepped on a mine. So they sent a doctor from Granada that was the person who did the abortions in the guerrilla camps. The doctor crashed and killed himself. As a second option, they called a *mafioso* from Villavicencio, and they were with these guys looking for ways to do terrorism. They did an attack to the water system in Villavicencio and other things along the way, and they put a bomb in the Caracol building, or they financed it. It was then that the army asked me to help them because they did not have an arrest warrant.

"So it was in working tightly with the army that we helped and made a prosthetic leg for this man, and that was what allowed the authorities to track these people and put them in jail. After they went to jail, they began to call me to ask for 250 million pesos and they threatened to declare against me in court if I didn't give them the money. They sent a note with a social worker from the jail.

---

13 Víctor Julio Suárez Rojas — a.k.a. Jorge Briceño Suárez was a high ranking member of the FARC.

We have her testimony. I also told this to the intelligence officers.

"That, Your Honor, is the sad situation in which we find ourselves today. And now this colonel from the 13th battalion launched this initiative, and no one found out about it until now."

The room was pretty quiet. I couldn't even believe he was saying all this out loud. In all my years, things like this had been a secret within walls that he would tell me every once in a while when he was not on his guard. Sometimes I would be with him when he would speak to both Colombian and American intelligence officers about what was going on in the war zones. They would roll out enormous maps and highlight specific areas where either the drug industry was growing wildly or where they thought there were hostages being held.

But now he was saying this in front of everyone, including about thirty reporters. Dad always told me, "We will help anyone who needs it, no matter who they are, only if it is to save their lives or the lives of others." And he has been true to his word. He will help anyone who needs help, whether it is a

wounded guerrilla, paramilitary, soldier, or a farmer. But he has always taken firm action against the drug trade and terrorism, no matter where it came from, risking his life and even his own family's lives.

Throughout my dad's speech, the prosecutor and the police officer had their mouths wide open. The judge listened intently and then gave Mónica the turn to speak. The judge still looked very stern.

Dad reading the Chronicles of Narnia to my little brother Dylan. When I was 7, Dad would give me an Oreo for every chapter I read. He taught us to love those books.

Dad showing a Richard Wurmbrand book to a family of farmers.

A soldier receives a book from my dad.
They usually all love reading.

Chapter 22
Mónica

MÓNICA TOLD ME later that this case was
specifically hard for her because she had lost
her objectivity as a lawyer. This time she was
not defending a stranger but someone she saw
as her own son or brother.

Mónica had her investigator read the
witness accounts and the newspaper articles
written about my dad's missionary work.

He began, *"New Herald* wrote a report in
2007, which said that the FARC wanted
to talk to officers in the army and not with
politicians. And this was a proposal of the
FARC to initiate contacts with good faith,
where the FARC sent this communication
with missionary Martín Stendal, and where
they highlight his missionary endeavors of
giving Bibles to guerrillas and paramilitaries
and military troops in various areas of
Colombia, among which is Sumapaz.

"Christian Magazine published 'A Pastor
of Peace in the Mouth of a Lion,' written

by Jorge Castellanos, where the missionary endeavors of Martín Stendal are highlighted, and it is also highlighted how the message of God is given to illegal groups and Indigenous tribes in various parts of the country.

"*Acts and Chronicles Magazine:* 'The Time to Forgive Has Come.'

"CBN news did a report on Colombia titled 'The Christian Light Fills the Dark Void in Colombia.'

"'The Caracol radio show, *Voices of Kidnapping,* directed by Herbín Hoyos, reported, 'Missionary Martín Stendal talks about his work and the distribution of radios and Bibles through a plane in the jungles of Colombia to guerrillas and paramilitaries.'"

The investigator read on with a few more articles; then it was Mónica's turn to speak.

Her voice trembled as she began.

"The work of this missionary is nomadic. It is not static like a priest at a church would be. The missionary goes from one place to another, and he is in a war zone."

Mónica's voice was like the sound of a mother defending her son. She was shaking.

It was all she could do to keep her quivering voice from cracking because of her suppressed tears.

"Get it together Mónica," my sister whispered.

"What does this missionary do?" Mónica continued. "The missionary has a spiritual and humanitarian job. The humanitarian work is not unlinked from the spiritual one. It cannot be unlinked because he is in a war zone. This help is directed toward individuals, and not to identified armed groups or political groups."

Mónica began to gain confidence.

"So he has done his work with farmers, soldiers, paramilitaries, and guerrillas. They are the people who are present in these areas in which he goes. His only preoccupation is to disarm the heart of the individual, not to disarm an armed faction, or to defeat some constitutional estate, or to bring down a legally established estate.

"The Ministry of the Interior has recognized his missionary endeavors. We see that there is a fundamental right of the freedom of worship and religion that is established in the 18th article of the Constitution – a right that every person has, not only the Colombian citizens, but also anyone living here.

"There is also a right to peace in the 22nd article of the Constitution. It has also been established that Mr. Martín Stendal has tried for the past thirty-some years as his personal battle to achieve a peace process. And we see entities from the Colombian government that have allowed him to enter into the country of Cuba for this peace process – to do a spiritual work. This work that he is doing there; he is doing it with the recognition of all the governmental testaments.

"It is mentioned here, and I want to emphasize it, that President Uribe in the year 2009, personally asked him to set up a radio station in less than twenty-four hours, in order to advise the citizens of Cajamarca regarding the volcano activity, because there were no radio stations that could warn the community. The president did this because of the same reports given to him by the generals in the army regarding his {Martín Stendal's}

missionary activities in the area and the capacity he has to install these radio stations in a brief amount of time.

"I mention all this to say that in this case, the crime of rebellion, as established in article 467 [of the Colombian criminal code], does not exist.

"As far as what the prosecutor said – that Martín represents a danger to society or to the victims – we see that the prosecutor has no evidence to prove this. How can we know that Martín represents a danger to society and to the victims? In this case we are confronted with a "crime" that is framed within the constitution of the state. In this case the passive subject [in other words, the victim] of this would be the state itself. So how could he put the state itself in danger if he is searching for peace processes? And he has helped legally established entities such as the army. They have publicly recognized him a number of times for the work he has done in the Armed Forces. These same activities he has done with other individuals, other actors in the conflict. This includes the giving of Bibles, of radios where the only frequencies that can be heard are the stations that give a Christian message. These radio stations have no other purpose.

"As for the third point, the prosecutor's concern that the person in question would not attend the due process: may I remind you, Your Honor, that it was Mr. Martín Stendal that presented himself to the police yesterday, in a voluntary manner, to clarify his situation because he knew he was being investigated. He carried all the evidence in that moment in order to explain his missionary work. So he is not interested, in any way, in avoiding this process. To the contrary, he is interested in clearing up his situation because he is nationally and internationally recognized as a missionary. He is not interested in blemishing his name. He is interested in clearing it. So this third point is without a foundation. And these are the subjective requisites for the imposition of the security measure.

"As far as the first point in article 310 [of the criminal code], the danger for the community with the continuation of the criminal acts or the probable link with

criminal organizations: this is not proven
by the prosecutor up until now. He cannot
talk about a link with criminal organizations
because the work of Martín Stendal is
the work of a missionary directed toward
individuals indiscriminately, no matter what
their political or social status is. He is not
interested in a specific criminal organization,
or whether it has to do with delinquents or
not, or people that live in the area, or farmers;
it could be anyone because it is about showing
the love of God to individuals."

For a brief second, the judge's stern face
turned to empathy. This was the only time
during the trial that her guard came down,
and before too many people had the chance to
notice, she quickly wiped a tear from her eyes.
In an instant, the firm demeanor was back
again. Stephen told me later that when he
saw this, he thought that for sure the case had
been won.

Mónica continued, "And this has been
endorsed by the same entities of the state
because it is a missionary, spiritual, and
humanitarian endeavor.

"As far as the 312th article that establishes the probable evasion of the due process because of the ability he [Martín] has to leave the country or to remain hidden: well, his same recognition both nationally and internationally as a missionary is what makes him secure his stay in the country in order to clarify in a trial his missionary activity. He is not interested in evading the process, and he has demonstrated this; yesterday he was captured when he presented himself voluntarily to the police. So Your Honor, I believe it is not necessary to impose this security measure.

"The right to liberty could be taken away in extreme cases. The two purposes for liberty to be taken away are: first to make sure that the person being tried attends and faces his situation, and also when it involves the safety of their victims. We see that in either case, these two objectives are not affected, because Mr. Stendal is willing to face this process. He is willing to take this to the end and to show his real work within this armed conflict.

"We have evidence in a video taken of General Barrero in the year 2013, not too long ago, in a meeting where majors were being promoted to colonels, where he publicly presented Martín Stendal. Let's remember that in that time, General Barrero was the commander of the Armed Forces. In this time, he presented Martín to all of his subordinates telling of the work that Martín has done in all the areas of Colombia, and he asked for the backing of all the military so that Martín could fulfill his work in the areas of conflict. There is a video of this. And General Barrero is willing to give his testimony in the trial. So we see that the need for a security measure does not exist because these objectives of facing the process and those objectives of protecting the victim, which in this case [the victim] is the state itself, are safe.

"Martín Stendal has no criminal record. He is fifty-nine years old and he has lived in Colombia for around fifty years. His family – his parents – were the first missionaries that came to the Kogi Indigenous community in Colombia. He and his family have a strong love for Colombia, and he is not interested in abandoning Colombia. He is interested in the work he is doing in Colombia for peace. So much that he is willing to risk his own life and his own freedom."

This whole time I had been intently looking at Mónica and the judge, but when I looked at the people around me, there was not a dry eye in the room.

Mónica wrapped up her argument, "Therefore I ask you, Your Honor, that the imposition of a measure would be in the form of house arrest, and not of jail; that is less invasive and would guarantee Martín Stendal's fundamental rights. This is my petition Your Honor. Thank you."

Chapter 23
Gabriella's Prayer

MY MOM was heartbroken when Mónica asked for house arrest. She had lived through a kidnapping already, and the only thing that gave her hope then was seeing the fruit of what happened during that time and the fruit that continues as a result. Her three inspirations were: her husband, Richard Wurmbrand and how the Lord used him in prison to minister to his inmates, and the Lord Jesus who gave it all, even his own soul.

This attitude from my parents was truly inspiring. Both of them, individually, came to the resolution that if this was God's will, then so be it. From his night in jail my dad prayed and told the Lord, "If a jail ministry is what you are sending me to, then I accept it." They would face anything, if it were the Lord's path for them.

My mom said to me one day as we reflected back on this, "Even though it was hard for everyone, I was willing to not have the easy way out. I knew that he would rather be with difficult people and talking to them about the Lord than buried in a house. And I prayed that all this would not be in vain – that it would be the Lord's will to light a revolution in those horrible jails of Colombia. It sounds cruel, but there are very needy people there, and the Lord cares for them. That is what gave me hope during the kidnapping, and that is what I was holding on to then."

When Mónica began describing Dad's ministry during the trial, Stephen could relate concerning what he had found: a home for the most unlikely people – because for the first time in his life, Stephen felt he had found his place in life, and now it was in danger of ending.

It is hard to put this into words, but more than books and Bibles, more than radio stations and sermons, what makes this extraordinary is this: as the Lord has chosen to reveal himself more and more to people of all backgrounds, they have found what they never knew before – a home. They have found their God-given place in life.

Sammy begged the Lord not to put Dad's face to shame before everyone. Moments before the trial, Sammy found Dad in the bathroom. They had about a thirty-second private meeting before the police walked in. My dad quickly handed Sammy his personal cell phone and told Sammy that he was now in charge of the family. Sammy had been overwhelmed at the thought of being like Peter, someone who denied the Lord Jesus in his worst hour. He asked the Lord if he could be like John instead: a disciple who stood with Jesus even in his moment of death.

Now as a confirmation that the Lord had answered his prayer, my dad had entrusted his entire family over to his son-in-law Sammy, something very similar to what Jesus did when he entrusted his mother Mary to John (John 19:25–27).

I asked the Lord to not let my dad go to jail. Mónica had told me before that each cell only has one small bunk bed, and because they don't have enough space, they fit twice as many people in there: instead of two men, they make space for four. Nothing could be more inhumane than this. She told me that this was why they did not allow anyone to bring cameras into prisons; they don't want anyone to find out about the serious human rights violations going on in there.

Before the hearing began, everyone was giving Mónica their advice. Hugo Tovar wanted Mónica to ask the judge for complete freedom. Mónica, on the other hand, said the best thing that could happen was that he be given house arrest. The worst thing that could happen was that he be sent to jail. Mom tried to tell Mónica to ask for jail instead of house arrest but she had lost her voice. Mom thought he would be terribly bored if stuck in the house for years. Dad told me later that fortunately for him, mom had tonsillitis that day which took her ability to speak away. Hence, she was not able to convey her opinion to the lawyers about Dad being sent off to jail ministry.

I fervently prayed for house arrest. My mom prayed for the Lord to bless a jail ministry. The prosecutor asked for my dad to be put through what would be a lengthy

trial under several charges that would result in sentences of at least fifteen years each in a maximum-security prison. The waiting time to establish an official trial date can take two or three years in Colombia, and there is no bail.

Thank God that he doesn't give us everything we ask for. To my great relief, the Lord had chosen to listen to the request of my nine-year-old niece instead.

The judge looked at both Mónica and the prosecutor and said, "The evidence against him is both insufficient and subjective. He is free! There will be no imputation of charges."

The night before, my niece Gabriella had prayed, "Lord, please release my grandpa from prison today, and please let our lives continue as normal tomorrow!" And that's exactly what would happen.

It was all we could do to contain our joy. The police guarding the courtroom summoned us out while my dad, the prosecutors, the lawyers, and the judge, continued inside.

Later on, when I spoke with Mónica after the hearing, she said, "I know I'm not the best lawyer. I know that those men out there are a lot better lawyers than me, but I was asking the Lord to use me because I am the weakest. And he did."

The outcome of the day was unexpected. We felt as if Colombia had won the world cup in soccer, and I think it won a lot more than that, that day. Countries are blessed, not by the greatness of their infrastructure, the abundance of their natural resources, or the beauty of their landscapes, but rather by the number of citizens that are whole-heartedly sold out to doing the Lord's will and accomplishing his purposes. People like Dad make Colombia a far greater nation as a result. After living there for most of his life, he had just recently been given his Colombian citizenship.

The press was waiting with lights and cameras for someone to interview. I was the first one to be interviewed, and I did not know it was all going out live on the air.

I said, "We can be grateful because today justice won in Colombia! Several guerrillas in jail were trying to extort my dad, and since he didn't pay them a cent, they declared against him. The news channel RCN needs to rectify its story or else it will lose all its credibility."

Someone yelled, "And Caracol needs to rectify their story too!"

"What do you think is the cause of all this?" one of the reporters asked.

"I don't know exactly," I said, "but it says in the Bible that the love of money is the root of all evil. I suppose it has something to do with that."

"Is your dad a false positive?" (This is a term used in Colombia when the army or the police takes someone who has nothing to do with the war and uses them to prove that they are obtaining "results" for the war.)

"Yes, he is a false positive."

"Does this affect the peace process?" they asked.

"Of course it affects the peace process," I replied, "because how can we have peace in Colombia when innocent people are being put in jail and ones who need to be inside are being let out?"

They tried to accuse my dad falsely and put him in jail, while in the meantime, his false accusers were released early because they had made declarations against my father.

After about half an hour, we were able to go inside the courtroom again, and this time my father was able to hug each one of us. The first one he hugged was my mom, and both of them cried as they embraced. Then he hugged my sister, Sammy, and others who were standing near. My dad said that as soon as the judge had declared him free, the prosecutor got very upset – more so than my dad had ever seen him before – and yelled for an appeal.

The judge told him to stop wasting the government's money and time on this case. We worked on this case for another two years and six months after that, just because the man made an appeal. In the Colombian justice system, the prosecutor is allowed to make an appeal, unlike with the American system.

My dad walked out and was soon faced with about a dozen reporters, cameras, and lights.

All his friends clapped and shouted as he left the courtroom and was immediately surrounded by journalists wanting to know his side of the story.

His first words were, "It was an education for me, and now I have more confidence in Colombia's justice."

One reporter said, "It was a tremendous injustice that was done to you."

My dad replied, "Look, we all need the love of God, and that is how we are going to have peace in Colombia." Everyone started to clap and cheer.

"What happened to you is a lot like what happened to you in the movie you made, *La Montaña?*"

"Yes," he replied, "sometimes you write things, and then you have to live the reality. Because we can't write a message of God without living it, and God's path is sometimes full of tribulations, but then there are moments of a lot of joy, and here we are, very happy."

The day before this trial, Dad had just finished writing the introduction to one of his books called *Queen Esther and the Ring of Power,* where he told the story of John Bunyan and how he had been working on *The Pilgrims Progress* but never found the time to write it until Bunyan was put in prison, and since he had no other distractions, he had finally finished it. Dad wrote that he did not want the Lord to have to put him in prison in order to finish writing all the books he had in his heart to write. Now a day later, he too, had been put in prison. Dad took it as a sign that he needed to desperately focus on writing the messages he had in his heart.

"Martín, it was a huge mistake, but do you forgive the authorities who did this to you?"

"Of course. Look, if we don't forgive, we won't be forgiven."

Big shouts of amen resounded as everyone clapped.

After a few more questions, a reporter asked, "What did you think when the

prosecutor said you were a threat to society and that since you have another citizenship, you should leave the country?"

"I'm not going to leave this country, and that is why I presented myself and faced this thing."

The reporter said, "You love Colombia."

"Yes, I love Colombia a lot." Dad smiled as he answered the question.

We went home, and thirty of our closest friends celebrated with us until about 2:00 a.m. eating, talking, and laughing. My brother's Alaskan malamute, Corin, yelped and whined when he saw my dad. He knew that this night away from home was unlike any other. I no sooner went to sleep when I began getting bombarded with phone calls. The press had gotten my phone number. Reporters wanted to interview my dad, and most of their talk shows began at 6:00 a.m.

Unbeknown to me, I thought these were serious journalists with no preconceived ideas in their minds and whose only intent was to discover the truth. While some of them were, a lot of them weren't. Many of them had already formed what they thought was the truth and their interviews sounded like another day in trial with the police investigator and the prosecutor. I regret having answered some of those calls and passing them to my dad.

In one day, many things that were hidden were brought to the light. In one day many friends we didn't know we had showed themselves and spoke up.

* * *

After the trial, I went to the jail once again to visit Jorge Pirata and all the other witnesses who were willing to testify in favor of Dad. This time, Juan Angarita our investigator, Mónica, and Stephen accompanied me. It was so beautiful to hear and see the witness of these former paramilitary commanders standing up for Dad in his darkest hour.

Chapter 24
B-pa's Passing

ABOUT TEN DAYS after my dad's trial, Grandma called to tell me that B-pa had passed away on March 1. In a sense, B-pa and Dad both went to jail on the same day. The hospital might as well be jail, only it's worse because your freedom is taken and on top of that, so is your health. Neither B-pa nor Grandma found out about dad's imprisonment until after his release.

B-pa, who had the habit of reading the newspaper every single day, did not read it that one day because of his fall, and there were no newspapers available in the hospital.

He struggled very hard for about nine days because they would not operate on him. Grandma fought very hard with every nurse, doctor, and secretary there to get them to operate on him as quickly as possible because she knew he wouldn't make it if they waited too long. But they said they couldn't operate right away because he had taken aspirin.

Meanwhile, the hospital was constantly filled with Kogis wanting to see their missionary. The nurses were so mortified by the new type of guests that they put a big sign on the door of his room saying "No Visitors Allowed." But Grandma left the door wide open so no one could see the sign.

In and out they came, causing a scandal in the Santa Marta Hospital. The scandal was that it was uncommon for so many Kogis to visit the hospital. They are very different from everyone else. Both men and women have long black scraggy hair and wear a completely white attire. Grandma went to talk to the nurses and told them they couldn't block the visitors because he was a missionary to them, and they had a right to see him. The head nurse said it was fine but that they had to stay far back and sit on the couch.

B-pa really didn't want to die. Becoming older and getting weaker with the passing years and realizing time was only getting shorter was something B-pa never took well to. Now he was fighting his very last battle here on earth, and he had Grandma and his

grandson Kaleb, along with the help of all his
Kogi friends, and from afar he had the prayers
of the rest of his family and friends to help
him through it.

"This is just another adventure. You always
like new adventures," Grandma said, trying to
encourage him one day at the hospital.

"Yeah, but I've never done it before,"
B-pa's weak, sad voice answered.

Grandma says she sang him all the old
songs they used to sing in their church in
Minnesota, back as a young couple before
they came to Colombia and before they even
had any children – hymns such as "My Home
Is in Heaven" and "This World Is Not My
Home."

A few months before, a book had arrived
for B-pa in the mail. A lady in the United
States had written a series of missionary
stories and in it was a story about B-pa. A
couple of strong men picked up the whole
bottom sheet of his hospital bed and lifted
him into a lounge chair. While he was sitting
in the chair and was awake, Grandma read
him this book. She got to the part where B-pa

prayed for a Kogi chief named Mama Nacio. As a result, this chief was healed miraculously from an infirmity that would have otherwise claimed his life. B-pa was a young, vibrant, and spirit-filled missionary in his thirties back when this happened. This miracle was what allowed their entrance into a tribe that had been closed to outsiders for centuries.

In all their years of missionary work with the Kogis, B-pa and Grandma never witnessed a Kogi burial because the Lord would always heal them or give Grandma and Grandpa the wisdom to know how to treat them, even though they weren't even doctors.

The mortality rate in that tribe while they were working there was nonexistent. They built a little airstrip up in the middle of the Sierra Nevada Mountains with the permission of all the tribal leaders. For years they worked on learning the Kogi dialect and figuring out an alphabet for them to be able to have their own written language. Grandma had taught many how to read, and B-pa translated their very first Kogi Bible.

Tears streamed down B-pa's face when Grandma read him his own story.

"You know, you really accomplished a lot in your life," Grandma encouraged him, "And you helped so many people. I've never met anybody who would go into debt to help a poor person, to help a person that needed an operation or with groceries and not just necessary groceries, you would buy them treats too."

"'The Lord always supplied,'" she later told me one day when we talked about Grandpa. "He had a generous heart, and that was from the Lord, because when I met him, he was an only child, and he was really selfish. If we ever needed to make a decision, he would pray, and in less than twenty-four hours he would have a word from the Lord. This word usually defied common sense.

One of the last days that he lived, I kept hearing words inspired by a verse from 2 Peter 1:11 'They will have a grand entrance into the kingdom of God.' Kaleb had a program in his computer that gave all the different translations. I went on it and looked up that verse and it said in one translation, 'God is planning a great welcoming party to welcome him.' I think that is what happened."

* * *

The doctors finally gave him the operation, but after he came back from it, my grandpa was never the same. He had a very bad night and called out to my grandma the whole time. The next day, the room was filled with Kogis, my grandma, and Kaleb. Every breath had become a huge struggle. The nurses took his vital signs and the doctor said, "It won't be long now."

A pastor that was in the room read a Psalm, and B-pa's breathing quickly returned to normal.

Grandma noticed that every time he took a breath, there was a bigger space in between. "Kaleb, he is going right now. We have to pray," she whispered.

He died with people praying for him in three different languages: Kogi, Spanish, and English. As wind blew into the stuffy hospital room, B-pa took his last breath. Everyone felt as if the angels had come and taken him.

Suddenly a change in his face came, and he wasn't a human being anymore, just a body.

After he died, Grandma was able to talk to the director of the hospital and tell him everything that had happened and how they had not operated on him in time. B-pa had to wait nine days for the operation, and he was too weak to wait that long. She gave the director B-pa's book *High Adventure in Colombia* and told him a little of their story in the country. When he had heard everything, he sighed and shook his head as if in regret, "Three days would have been enough. We had a grand character here, but we treated him like a tourist."

Grandma Pat wrote this a few days later to remember the details of his parting:

"He had a radiance in his face that increased. He looked like he was already seeing glorious things. He never did open his eyes again, but his breathing just got slower and slower until it stopped. I didn't let them resuscitate him. As he passed, Kaleb and I prayed in English, then Amanda in Spanish, and Alberto, a Kogi Christian, in

Kogi. As soon as his spirit was gone, the glory departed, and within an hour his earthly body was just a cold, grey corpse. I didn't want to look again.

"Alberto called friends, and soon the hospital room filled with Kogis. They started planning the burial at once. I found out they had been praying for a year that he would come back to Santa Marta so that they could bury him up on their land. He was buried as a *Kogi mama* (a spiritual leader). We will put up a tombstone saying in Spanish and Kogi that he was the first missionary to bring the Word of God to the Kogis."

B~pa helping mama Nacio.

Grandma and Grandpa

Chapter 25
A King's Burial

DAD, STEPHEN and I used the tickets we had already purchased months before, which turned out to be set for the exact dates to attend B-pa's funeral.

The snowcapped mountains of the Sierra Nevada, where Grandma and Grandpa had lived and worked for years, pierced through the clouds, giving us a magnificent view on our forty-five-minute flight there. They looked so tall that it felt as if the 30,000-foot elevation of the plane was just as high as them. B-pa always told me that the Sierra Nevada of Santa Marta was unique in that it was the highest coastal mountain range in the world.

Soon we were landing in the small airstrip of Santa Marta. The wonderful blue of the Caribbean Ocean adorned on the side with yellow sand and beautiful green trees was now in full view. The captain hit the brakes of the plane really hard as soon as we touched the

ground in order to make it in time without crashing into the airport terminal. Every time I land there, I always think they should make the airstrip at least a little longer so that the big 737 Boeing planes don't have to brake so hard, and so I don't have to pray so much. Also, I am always surprised to see that the brakes of the plane are working well, and I thank God for I can live another day. The smell of salt, the feeling of the wind coming from the mountains and the sea, the warmth on my skin, and the wonderful view of the ocean make me even more grateful to be alive.

Our first stop before going to our hotel was Grandma's little apartment next to the sea. She was doing surprisingly well, given the circumstances. Grandma has always been a strong lady. Nothing ever seemed to dampen her spirits. The bright and happy smile was on her face as usual, making her just as beautiful as ever.

Grandma was a knockout when she was younger. She could have been one of those actresses with the timeless beauty from the 1940s and '50s, like Ingrid Bergman was, with the beautiful curly mid-length brown hair, the classic delicate nose, and the great smile. Now, as an older woman in her eighties, she looked just as pretty because she hadn't lost the smile, and her wrinkles were smiling wrinkles.

Years before, on their sixtieth wedding anniversary celebration up in Minnesota, one of the things my aunt said about her was that even in the tribe, hiking up the mountain with mud up to her knees and not having a lot to eat as far as protein, sugar, or any of the comforts you would have in America, she never lost her staple smile. Many times the only protein they had was one egg, and Grandma would use it wisely and make everyone a chocolate cake in her portable missionary oven in order to distribute the few grams of real nutrition among everyone. Tears had streamed down B-pa's face when he was reminded of all this at the celebration.

Now, B-pa had died, and Grandma was still smiling.

The Kogis did not let Grandma do anything for his burial. They told her they

would take care of every detail. The next day, they had a bus pick us all up, and we drove for three hours up the unpaved mountain road only stopping once for refreshments at a little town on the foothills of the Sierra Nevadas. No one wore black. Mostly everyone was dressed in colors or in white like the Kogis. I wore a beautiful yellow dress, typical of the folkloric style that Cuban farm girls used to wear in the 1950s, and a white straw hat.

Grandma wore a white shirt with a beautiful big straw hat decorated with little flowers. She looked radiant. My aunts and uncle (Dad's siblings) and all my cousins made it feel more like a nice family outing, as opposed to a funeral. The bus was packed to the limit, and I was in the very back, which made me get claustrophobic for a minute, but fortunately I regained my composure.

Up the mountain we went, singing songs and telling jokes. It was a wonderful reunion. Soon we arrived at the little town where all the Kogis were waiting for us.

Eight strong Kogi men carried B-pa's casket up the mountain. Kogi children, women, men, and *mamas* (leaders) walked

closely behind, while two other Kogis helped
Grandma on her way up the hill. They
brought a chair so she could sit and rest
whenever she needed a break. Up we went
until we came to a beautiful view of the valley
and the mountain range.

There, many other Kogis awaited our
arrival with a delicious feast of wild chicken
and soup. The casket was put in the center of
what would be the place of the ceremony in
the great and beautiful outdoors.

Each one of B-pa's children spoke of him.

"I didn't know that everyone didn't live
with miracles each day. To me it was just
life. It was all because of my dad," my aunt
Sharon, his first daughter, said of him.

My aunt Gloria said, "I learned what it's like
to have an anointing of God over a person's
life that changes everything. Living up here in
the Sierra with B-pa was like living with Jesus
and his disciples. B-pa was anointed to preach
and heal – to show love where sometimes it
was difficult. He had a special anointing to love
the Kogis that probably nobody had ever had
before in their lives. They finally felt love from
someone, and probably many of them for the

very first time in their life. That is probably the biggest legacy."

Alfonso, one of the Kogis who had been raised by my grandparents, spoke next. "To me, he is a person that was valuable. And he stayed here… in the Sierra."

Another Kogi read a verse in their language from the Bible B-pa had spent years translating for them: "I have fought the good fight." Even though I couldn't understand what he was saying I could feel his emotion and knew the part of the Bible he was reading. Soberly and with conviction he continued, "I have finished the race. I have kept the faith. From now on, there is laid up for me a crown of righteousness, which the Lord, the righteous judge, shall give me in that day, and not to me only but unto all those who have loved his appearing" (2 Timothy 4:7–8).

Cesar Trigos, our brother who was one of the many children who had been raised and adopted by my grandparents and who had sung at our wedding reception, said with tears in his eyes and heartfelt conviction:

"They weren't the missionaries of fifteen days or a month. They were the missionaries of a lifetime. There is a seed that is not going to die. And the gratitude I have is that before the Lord and before you, I will live a life for the Lord."

I sang a few hymns that I knew B-pa had liked, and after that my dad spoke and ended the ceremony with a prayer: "We ask Lord that through the mountains of Colombia there would be an impartation of my dad's missionary spirit. We ask that more missionaries would be born within all the groups, with the same vision, with the same drive, with love of righteousness, with spirit and sacrifice. We ask this in the name of our Lord Jesus Christ. Amen."

Soon we all walked further up the mountain, with the eight Kogi men carrying the casket, to bury my grandpa.

It was the Kogi tradition to never let any dirt fall on the casket of a *Kogi mama,* which means "chief." What they do is they dig out a crypt through the soil and rock on the top of a mountain. They dig straight down for about eight or more feet and then go sideways for

three or four feet. This is where they place the body. Then they cover the part leading into the crypt with dirt and debris, leaving the casket in a cave underneath the ground with nothing touching it, only a ceiling that is rock and earth.

Kogi children surrounded the hole and sang old Christian hymns in their language while the men placed B-pa's body inside the cave. Every Kogi child, woman, and man took a flower and dropped it inside the earth beside the casket.

"There will be no need for the light or its brilliance," they sang in Kogi as they each dropped a flower into the earth. "The sun will no longer shine, nor give its heat." A cute little five-year-old Kogi girl smiled as she sang along with everyone else and dropped her flower, "There will be no crying, nor sadness, nor pain, because Jesus, the King of Heaven will always be our comforter."

Later, as we were heading down the mountain to get into the bus that would take us down to the city of Santa Marta again, a Guambiano Indigenous leader from the other side of the country in Cauca called Dad on the phone to comfort him, for he had heard about the arrest and his father's funeral. "Don't worry Martín, if anything ever happens to you, we have a plot of land here in our mountains that we have reserved specifically for your burial." Dad smiled. The Guambianos had meant to comfort him by making sure he knew he would receive the highest honors from them when he died. But it was still a little too soon for Dad to have others already planning his funeral.

Kogi friends carry B-pa's casket up the mountain.

Singing at B-pa's burial.

Chapter 26

No Turning Back

IF THE JUDGE had not let Dad free, who knows how long he would have been in jail until we were finally able to clear his name and prove his innocence. It would have all been over that very night if the prosecutor had not made an appeal. But because he made an appeal, it took us almost three years to win the case.

For one month after the hearing, I worked hard every day on Dad's defense, until one day I felt in my heart that I should not focus on that anymore. Mónica and Juan were meant to do that job. I was meant to do something else, and I knew this was becoming nothing but a distraction. The investigator came one day to ask me to make videos and find and translate articles for the case, but I told him a simple no. He was shocked.

In April of 2015, Lisa and I began writing another script based on how beautiful and free Colombia had been before all the drug

266

trade started, and how swiftly and negatively the country changed as a result. Several things happened during this time: my mom and dad grew up in the Eastern side of the country which had been a haven free from all the heavy production of marijuana, coca and opium. Soon the produce of all this would begin to darken everything. They were married, and Dad was kidnapped for five months by terrorists that financed themselves with these narcotics. Noel, (the main guerrilla leader in our film *La Montaña* and the one who Dad referred to in his defense) was raised to be a guerrilla and became one of Dad's captors.

As the production of these drugs continues now in more force than ever before, this movie may be timely. We felt inspired to write the script but the making of it will be when the Lord says, as everything else has been.

Some people say, "Please, not *another* movie on war and drugs!" And it's true, too many dark movies have been made on these issues. But there are two reasons as to why this film would be different: 1. Most of the other movies bring no hope or solutions. 2. We have not yet overcome this epidemic, and it is deeply and negatively affecting our world.

Now the Indigenous people in Cauca are being confronted with a test once again. Different terrorist groups, as well as people inside the government are coaxing them into producing cannabis (or legal marijuana). They are misleading them to believe that this will all be used for health and pharmaceutical products.

Someone once said, "History does not repeat itself but it often rhymes." Sammy called Marco Tulio, the Páez leader, and told him to beware because people in the government may try to persuade them to plant marijuana. Marco Tulio replied, "It's not the first time they've tried to make us do something like that. Years ago, they tried to get us to plant opium."

The truth of the matter is that the production of these drugs have only caused desolation and death in these areas.

This movie would inspire people everywhere to stand up against this evil once

and for all. Because when people see the example of others standing firm no matter what the circumstances were, as both my maternal and paternal grandfathers did a long time ago, they may find the courage to do likewise.

We also began dreaming of making another movie based on the Great Awakening in the 1900's with the loggers of northern Minnesota. The United States of America would not be the country it is now without the three Great Awakenings the Lord gave her. But those happened years ago and the truth of the matter is that America desperately needs another Great Awakening. I see this as the only solution for a true turn of the tide.

We finished writing the script about Colombia in my grandparents' cabin in Minnesota, and we also began looking at the sets for the logging camps that would make part of this wonderful story about Frank Higgins and the loggers.

Lisa and I both became pregnant during this time. Nine months later, I had the cutest blue-eyed son named Noah (just as my mom had said) and Lisa had girl and boy twins: a handsome red-haired boy named Miles and the most beautiful little curly haired girl named Kate Mae. Miles, Kate, and Noah were all born in 2016 during the month of January, only twelve days apart.

For most of my life I thought it was a given that my first son would be named Noah. What I did not take into account was that my husband might not have the same opinion. For seven months of pregnancy we argued about it. Over and over again, I would tell Stephen that Noah was my favorite Bible story and my favorite name. He, in turn said he had grown up with too many Noah's in his life and was tired of it. I was determined but nothing I said could convince him.

That is until I told him the story of when my mom read me Psalm 23 for my 23rd birthday and said that one day I would have a wonderful husband and a son named Noah. Then I pulled out the necklace she had given me with the word 'Noah' engraved on it. He

shrugged his shoulders and said, "Well, how can I compete with that!"

I don't think I would have won the debate if my mom hadn't done that.

Looking back, I know that Lisa and I would have never planned to become pregnant had our dad still been in jail. We would have postponed our plans for making other movies as well until he was released.

Stephen and Sammy started off with providing one water purifying system for the Páez Indians that I wrote about in chapter 10. Who would have thought that this would multiply and that hundreds of communities all along the countryside would require these same water systems? The Lord placed it in Stephen's heart to work full time in these projects.

After Stephen's trip to Zambia with my dad and brothers (in which he began talking to me like a man with a vision), we began dreaming of a radio station for Africa. Surprisingly enough, more than 50% of the population on that continent speak English. Soon after we married, Stephen and I began our very first English speaking radio station. All of the other radio stations we've worked on in Colombia have been in Spanish. It is a very pleasant way to listen to the English Jubilee Bible while also listening to good music. For now, people in Africa and elsewhere can hear it if they download the app called Jubilee Radio. But someday the Lord may provide a way to broadcast it on AM, FM, or shortwave frequencies in this part of the world.

On February 28 of 2018, our second son, Lincoln, was born. Lincoln means Roman colony by the lake. It is interesting that soon after I had Lincoln, the land of the 10,000 lakes opened up to us in a whole new way. During the time I was pregnant, Lisa was inspired to write the story of Frank Higgins and the Great Awakening for a movie script. Soon after Lincoln was born, we all went to Minnesota to scout out locations and create contacts for this new film. If the Lord allows us to make this movie, we will have become the Roman colony by the lake, just because we are from Colombia, a Roman Catholic

country, and in order to film it, we will have to live next to one of those many lakes.

So the Lord in his goodness gave us all the ability to continue his will. Many other people would have been affected as well because Dad does not only have his immediate family, but hundreds of other families that love and care for him in Colombia.

There were still difficulties afterward. We received many threats. Not only were these threats aimed at Dad, but at our whole family, and toward anyone who listened to his teachings or read his books. Terrible letters written by psychopaths would arrive in our mail. Whoever was behind the letters wanted him to retract and not fight for his innocence anymore, or else, they said, they would kill him and his family.

Three of the four witnesses that testified against Dad in court disappeared. They suddenly vanished from the prison system. A general who is a friend of ours says they were most likely shot, giving me reason to believe there was much more behind this arrest than the simple story of false witnesses wanting extortion money. Maybe we will never find out what wickedness was really behind the whole thing. So wicked that they did not hesitate in resorting to murder in order to get rid of the evidence. Such evil is more than what my heart and mind can comprehend. (Carrillo, the last false witness was killed – shot twice in the head – in July of 2019.)

The situation in the country got exponentially worse. Now a kidnapping didn't seem so bad. There were worse, far more vile things going on. Many of Dad's friends were kidnapped, but now instead of negotiating for the release of the person, the family of the person kidnapped would have to negotiate to retain what was left of the corpse.

But somehow, it was okay for us. We continued our life as the Lord had given it to us, and everything seemed normal. Perhaps we were in an invisible bubble made for us by angels.

In January of 2017, First Step Forum[14] awarded Dad the Shahbaz Bhatti Freedom

---

14 The First Step Forum was formed in January 2002. It began with a gathering of a group of ambassadors, religious

Award[15] for his work promoting religious freedom. This international freedom of religion award had been given to Pope Francis previously. We received pictures of the pope with the prize in the Vatican. A letter said, "Please choose the time and the place of your award ceremony."

Dad chose the place where he had been preaching for the last seventeen years, teaching a different chapter of the Bible every Sunday. He never wanted a church, only a place where he could freely record his sermons for the radio stations and where anyone could go and listen to it. That is why the meetings were always in the evenings, so people wouldn't have to miss their regular morning church services. We had wanted

---

liberty experts, members of parliament, and members of the media in Berlin, Germany. The multinational gathering founded the First Step Forum as an initiative to monitor religious and human rights abuses worldwide with the goal of addressing potential problems before they become major events.

15 The award is named after Pakistan's first Christian Cabinet Minister who was murdered in 2011 for criticizing Pakistan's blasphemy laws.

Dad to pick a more beautiful auditorium to celebrate in, but he insisted that he wanted to share this moment with the people that had faithfully listened to him throughout all these years. Our good friends Bill and Mary Ann Bennett, who had faithfully prayed for all of us, supporting our ministry for years, came to witness Dad's award ceremony, and our mission representative in the USA, David Witt also came.

Lisa, Alex, and I decorated the drab auditorium with flowers and Christmas lights. By the end, we had transformed it into something beautiful. It seemed like a completely different venue, looking bright, colorful, and crisp. A Steinway grand piano was placed in the center of everything for Frank Fernández, the world-renowned Cuban pianist. I never knew a piano concert could stir my soul in such an immeasurable way.

Then Dad got up to speak. Despite the fact that there had just been a piano concert such as I had never heard before and the place was prettier than usual, Dad continued with the service as he did every Sunday; he preached from the next chapter of the Bible that was

due that day. His sermons stir my heart and my soul even more than any piano concert could.

And then the award was given to him. The first person he thanked when he had a chance to speak after receiving it was Fernando Torres. "Could Fernando Torres, my friend who has always stood beside me in the good and the bad times, please stand?" Our humble, kind, lifelong friend Fernando Torres stood up and everyone clapped loud and long.

I was reminded of the last movie in the *Lord of the Rings* trilogy, *The Return of the King,* when everyone gets back from winning the final battle, and Aragorn, the legitimate king of Gondor is finally crowned. The four small, seemingly insignificant hobbits bend to bow down to the new king.

But King Aragorn stops them with his hand and says, "My friends, you bow to no one." And Aragorn bows instead, and the whole kingdom follows his lead and bows. The only ones left standing are the four hobbits.[16]

---

16 The Return of the King is the third and final volume of

That part always made me cry because it reminded me of all the little people that never get recognized, but who always save the day. The world is a better place because of those small people, yet no one knows it. But our good King does. He recognizes and honors those little people who have fought alongside him in the battle, even if they are nameless and insignificant to the rest of the world.

It would be typical for my absent-minded dad to forget to thank all the countless others who have stood beside him through thick and thin, so as the people were distracted with clapping, Russell Jr. (who is a very thoughtful person) ran to Dad to whisper the name of a person he needed to thank in his ear. Then when the clapping died down, Dad thanked them and the clapping regained momentum again. Russell ran once again and whispered another name into his ear.

This went on, until pretty much everyone who needed to be thanked was thanked. Missionary Bruce Olsen was there. He was one

---

J. R. R. Tolkien's The Lord of the Rings (1955) on which the movie is based.

of my grandpa's favorite missionaries, and my dad also thanked him. Bill, Mary Ann, and David also were thanked for all their support from the USA for Dad's ministry.

Afterwards, our family had a small celebration with only our closest friends up on a terrace overlooking the city. Sammy and Lisa decorated it nicely with Christmas lights and had a great banquet waiting for everyone. Then came my turn to speak. I usually speak as our dad taught us to, from the heart, without having written anything down first. But this time I had a speech written out for myself. The night before, I hadn't been able to sleep until I wrote down what was in my heart to say. I still have it in my files today as a result. I began to read it out loud to everyone.

> After all the adventures we have lived through with Dad, I am reminded of the movie *The Lord of the Rings*,[17] our family favorite, when Sam urges Mister Frodo to continue on the task at hand that only he can do.

17 The Lord of the Rings is a film series of three epic fantasy adventure films directed by Peter Jackson, based on the novel written by J. R. R. Tolkien.

"I know. It's all wrong," says Samwise to Frodo, "By rights we shouldn't even be here. But we are. It's like in the great stories, Mr. Frodo. The ones that really mattered. Full of darkness and danger they were, and sometimes you didn't want to know the end. Because how could the end be happy? How could the world go back to the way it was when so much bad happened? But in the end, it's only a passing thing, this shadow.

"Even darkness must pass. A new day will come. And when the sun shines it will shine out the clearer. Those were the stories that stayed with you. That meant something. Even if you were too small to understand why.

"But I think, Mr. Frodo, I do understand. I know now. Folk in those stories had lots of chances of turning back, only they didn't. Because they were holding on to something."

"What are we holding on to, Sam?" Frodo asked.

"That there's some good in this world, Mr. Frodo. And it's worth fighting for."

I looked up from my paper to find Lisa, Russell, Dad, and Mom all crying. My brother Dylan would have been crying too had he been there, but he was off in Belize getting a degree in welding. What can I say? That movie moves all of us because with all we have lived through here, we can all relate. I continued with my speech:

In the past, there have been lots of chances of turning back, only Dad never did. When I was eleven years old, the missionary school in Bogotá that I attended was suddenly swarmed with missionary kids fleeing the violence of the Eastern Plains. Ray Rising had been kidnapped, causing more than three hundred missionaries to evacuate their base in Lomalinda. The nearby town of Puerto Lleras had been bombed and lay in ruins. Churches were destroyed. So many

pastors were killed in this part of
Colombia that it quickly became
the country with the most martyred
pastors in the world, according to
VOM statistics.

It was under these intense
circumstances that my dad bought
three of the missionary homes that
were left behind and decided to move
our little family out there.

The threat of guerrillas,
paramilitaries, or soldiers visiting or
ransacking our houses was constant.
I still remember one remarkable dark
night. The power had gone out. In a
war zone, a power outage meant that
somebody had bombed an electricity
tower.

That dark, windy night, we lit
a candle and sat around our old
wooden table. The neighbor came
to tell Dad of all the terrible things
that were happening in the area,
giving him good reason as to why we
should leave. My dad pondered for a

moment. Then he looked at the candle with determination in his eyes and said, "There is still a small light that burns here, left from years and years of missionary work, ever since my dad and Uncle Cam arrived. I am not going to let that light go out."

"So we stayed, and miraculously we were given our very first radio station. Many more came after that. Years later, the reports we heard from people that had suffered a kidnapping were astounding. All of them said that the radio station was the only beacon of light they had had during their long years of captivity.

Then a general in the army gave Dad a riverboat called the *She Devil* that had belonged to the guerrillas. Dad painted it up and renamed it, *The Light of the Truth*. With all the friends and family that decided to go with him, he launched down river with the boat full of Bibles, Christian literature, and little

Galcom radios, which were fixed tuned to our radio stations.

People all along the shores came to greet the voyagers and waved little white handkerchiefs or white shirts. They had heard the boat was loaded with Bibles and it was their peaceful way of urging them to continue on their journey and also of getting a Bible. However, only a few days into their trip, in the town of Puerto Rico, the boat exploded, burning everyone's belongings except for the Bibles, the literature, and the radios.

Not more than a few minutes after it exploded, the guerrillas launched an attack from the other side of the river on the army that was protecting the town. My family had to run for cover. Soldiers kept them safe, as bullets miraculously ricocheted off of the gas pumps.

Russell Jr. (age twelve) became lost in the midst of all the confusion, and someone said he was by the shore of

the river where all the shooting was taking place. Dad lost his wits for a moment and attempted to go out to look for him. But his family held him down against his will and stopped him from going out. After the shootout was over, what a miracle it was to find that one of the families in the town had hidden Russell Jr. in a water tank. Tears rolled down everyone's faces when they found him safe and sound.

Again, this was the moment in which any other person would have said, "It's time to go home now. It's getting pretty dangerous." At least that is what everyone on the boat thought he would do. Fercho Alarcon who had been so shaken with everything that had happened, overheard Dad talking to another crew member that night of the tragedy, "We need to repaint the boat first thing in the morning, then we will continue on down river. I am taking Fercho and whoever else wants to go."

I am sure Fercho didn't sleep that night.

Then the time of the planes came. Missionary aviation had been dead for fifteen or maybe even twenty years. Until one day, the Lord provided a small two-passenger plane. Dad would fill this plane with the small parachutes that ladies in Canada and the USA had sewn. Tied to these parachutes were books, Bibles, and the Galcom radios tuned to our radio stations.

I had the wonderful opportunity of accompanying him one day with my camera ready to film everything. But Dad told me, "Leave your camera behind. I want to show you something."

I put my camera down and we took off from the gravel runway in the little airplane. Not more than five minutes later, we were flying over vast amounts of coca fields. Little farmhouses covered the landscape here and there. As soon as the people heard the sound

of the plane flying real low, they would run out of their houses waving white pieces of fabric as a sign of peace and welcome.

Then Dad would fly so low that it felt as if we could almost touch the rooftops of these farmhouses, and as soon as he was as low as he could get, he would turn the plane sideways so that his window was facing the floor of the earth and drop a little parachute down to the people.

We flew over a soccer field where there were two teams playing against each other. As soon as they heard the sound of the plane, they stopped their game and took their shirts off to wave them to us. This was the sign that they also wanted the little parachutes full of books and Bibles dropped onto them. Dad flew low and dropped them a couple of parachutes. They landed safely on the field.

This continued over and over again as we flew over all the landscape.

It was one of the most magical experiences I had ever had.

Dad was right to have me leave the camera. Such moments could never be captured fully and should only be lived fully. Soon he took me back home again and dropped me off. He took off one last time to deliver more parachutes.

About an hour later, he landed once again on the little rustic airstrip. This time, the plane was full of bullet holes. Dad was miraculously still alive. They had just missed him. But the plane was in bad condition. Guerrillas had shot at him and he had gotten out barely in time. Feeling scared for my dad's life, I thought for sure now was the time when he would say something like, "I guess we shouldn't do this anymore. We might get killed."

Instead, he took out his cell phone and called his brother up who was in the States, "Chaddy, will you order me some night vision goggles? Some

guerrillas just shot my plane, and I think the only solution will be to deliver the parachutes at night when they can't see me."

Soon, the night vision goggles arrived and he was making flights out of Lomalinda at four in the morning, so the enemy couldn't see him.

Throwing a parachute out of the plane.

Then, he was arrested, and the press accused him falsely of being a FARC guerrilla leader, attempting to ruin his reputation. Yet he decided to give them the chance to rectify their story and didn't sue them if they would correct it.

Ernesto, our Jewish friend who had prophesied that I would marry Stephen had a dream the morning after Dad was arrested. He heard a voice that said that Martín was not going to prison because the Lord needed him somewhere else. This proved to be true because he was released that night and soon we were sailing to Cuba from Florida. The Lord needed my dad over there instead. I continued my speech,

> After two months of my dad and Stephen working hard to get a sailboat fixed and ready for the trip to Cuba, we were finally able to set sail on the 3rd of August of 2015. The captain of *The Dawn Treader* was my dad. The first mate was Stephen. His little helper was my fifteen-year-old brother, Dylan. As for me, all I could do was sit and watch the endless ocean and remind God every once in a big wave that I was four months pregnant with our first

son and therefore to not let any serious storms hit us.

I'm sure God took note because a huge storm was over Havana when we were only hours away. We had two options: one was to turn east to the Florida Keys, avoiding the dense clouds ahead, or the other was to continue going south directly toward the storm and our destination.

The captain of our ship decided to continue south – on to Cuba. As the waves got stronger and stronger during the night, they shook the boat up and down, and the rain began to pour; all I could do was pray for morning to come quickly.

When I woke up the next day, the sun was shining, there was not a menacing cloud in the sky, and Havana could be seen in the far distance. I had never seen such a happy captain before. We could have turned back to Florida, but the captain of the ship was determined, and the Lord cleared the skies for us.

There were many chances of turning back, only Dad never did because he was holding on to something: "That there is some good in the world and it is worth fighting for."

The following is a musical account of all the adventures our family and friends have lived through in these many years of service to our Lord and to our beautiful country of Colombia."

Óscar Arias and his Mariachi band (the same artist that had performed at my wedding reception) gave us all a wonderful concert and sang all of the songs that had been written and recorded in our small home-recording studio throughout the years – songs about all the things God had done in the midst of the war and the violence.

First, Óscar sang a song written about Dad's kidnapping back in the '80s and how God used that to reach his captors with a new message. Then he went on to sing the songs

he had written of our adventures on the boat –
called *The Light of the Truth* – in the rivers of the
countryside. Violins, trumpets, and oversized
guitars accompanied his great voice. The
memories of this song move most of us to tears.

Don't Cry Anymore Colombia

Lord Jesus Christ
I beg you for Colombia
My beloved homeland
Is in mourning.
Innocent blood
Is spilled everywhere
Let this dirty war end now.

And our brothers
Are sacrificing themselves
For our Colombia
In search of peace.

Let us look onward
Orphans and widows
Let us unite our strength
As a symbol of peace.
The people of the countryside
And desolate towns

Drowning in the silence
Longing for happiness.

Don't cry anymore Colombia
Hope is rekindled
Through the rivers of this country
The peace boat sails
Russell and his friends
On board the ship
Are bringing the faithful message
With the "Light of the Truth."

Let us all implore together
Kneeling before Christ
With love and reverence
For our native nation.

Then he sang the songs about the adventures in the mountains of the country when two enemies decided to make peace with one another. These, he had written specifically for our film, *La Montaña,* which means "The Mountain." Óscar ended the presentation with a song he wrote when the government imprisoned Dad for supposedly being "Alias, 'the Gringo' of the FARC."

God Walks with the Gringo

Mister President,
It is you I'm speaking to today,
With all due respect, I tell you:
I don't know about laws,
I have not seen myself in courts,
But you must know who
Russell Martín Stendal is!
He is no traitor,
as the government affirms.

At the top of my lungs,
I shout, That God walks
shoulder to shoulder
with the gringo!

Tireless warrior
of a foreign cause
He exposes his life
in camps of war
It is not his fight,
but he fights anyway.

Today, shame fills my face
Because of the injustice of this nation.
They free bandits
and oppress their heroes;

No Turning Back

They are evildoers,
taking the innocent to trial,
staining their names.

You speak of peace in Habana,
but true peace
is not won with bullets
And those who do know how to fight
get their wings cut off.

"These are my friends!" Óscar exclaimed as
he pointed to all of us. My family and all our
friends who had been alongside us through
thick and thin all clapped and prodded him on.
He continued with another song:

I am going to sing for a group of people
That are worth a lot
Their leader is a great man
An exemplary patriot
Mister Martín Stendal

With his family at his side
They have given conquests
To this beautiful Colombia
Together they do great things
Give them an applause!

May it stay forever in history!
"A change of the heart"
Is the motto of this campaign

Lisa, Samuel,
Stephen, and Alethia,
Fernando Alarcon,
Alex Ramirez,
Russell Jr. and Dylan
With the backup from above
Have been forging
Better paths.

Marina, his wife, always smiling
Gives us an incentive
That we feel in our soul.

These are my friends!
I truly do love you
I will say it singing!

All of you have given me love
Sincere love from your hearts
That is why I carry you here in my chest
And in my songs!

Dad, Mom and their six grand-children.

No turning back always made Dad happy.

Chapter 27
Lisa's Painting

MY MOTHER has always told me that she does not want me to bring her any flowers for her funeral. She says, "Bring them to me while I am still alive, so I can enjoy them. What good are they to me when I'm dead?"

We were able to honor her life when she turned fifty. We planned a great surprise party for her and bought her a nice dress to wear for it. We made a fake invitation saying that a general from the army invited her and dad to a banquet and wanted them to come formally dressed in white. Beforehand, she had seen a white dress in a store that she really liked but never had the excuse to buy. That is why we said in the invitation that she had to be dressed in white.

When she read the dress code out loud to us, Lisa and I both exclaimed, "Oh mom! You should get yourself that white dress you've always wanted!"

And so she did – for the "event with the
generals." We invited all her closest friends
and family and all waited expectantly for her
at a ballroom we had reserved in a nice army
base in Bogotá. The tables were set as if it
were a wedding. We had her favorite band
of *llanera* music waiting to play. This is harp
music original to the Eastern Plains of the
country where she is from. She walked into
the ballroom expecting to find the boring
setting of army officials and other random
people. Was she ever happy to see her mom,
her sisters, and all of her friends instead! We
had a wonderful, and fun-filled night. Never
had we seen her so happy.

* * *

A few years later, we had the opportunity
of honoring dad with the Shahbaz Bhatti
Freedom Award ceremony. We also were
able to honor my sister Lisa with a Narnia
party after she and our friend and co-worker
Fernando Alarcón spent ten years working
on extraordinary radio plays in Spanish.
These audio books have blessed thousands of

kids and adults in the war-torn areas of this country.

Stephen and I made a Narnia themed costume party for Lisa with one of those great banquets that Aslan would make for his sons and daughters in *The Chronicles of Narnia* books. There was everything from cakes, and pies, to turkey, fruit, candy, mashed potatoes, corn on the cob, and even Turkish Delight. I was thankful to once again be able to honor someone while they are still alive.

Before the celebration, I had been wondering what to give Lisa as a gift for all of her hard work. Stephen told me I should have an artist paint a story from Narnia for her. Now that was a good idea!

We hired a painter and I gave him a picture I had found on the internet of Aslan the Lion standing with Jill Pole at the edge of the cliff, from where she had just caused her friend Eustace to fall. This story is found in the fifth book of the *Chronicles of Narnia* called *The Silver Chair*. I told the painter the meaning of the story and how Aslan represented God.

After three weeks of hard work, the painter finally had the finished draft of his work for me. Excited, I went over to pick it up, but to my dismay, I found he had depicted Aslan in a horrible way. The Lion's eyes looked fiery red and hateful. There was no mercy in them for Jill's mistake. It took me a few minutes to realize that this was probably the way he saw God, and that is why he had painted Aslan this way.

In the nicest way I could manage, I tried to explain to him how God was loving and kind and how he needed to portray that in the Lion's face, even though the girl had obviously not deserved it.

"Okay, I will do my best," he said.

A few days later, he sent me a picture of the new Aslan. This time I was even more mortified! Now, instead of a heartless and unrelenting Lion, he had painted a stupid one, a face that said, "Anything goes".

"Okay," I thought, "how do I get the idea of who God is across to him?"

He is a good Lion, but that does not mean he is a tame Lion, much less, a stupid one.

He forgives us, but that does not mean there are no consequences for our actions. He loves us, but he also hates our sinful nature. He is patient with us for a while, but there will come a time when he will demand maturity and nothing less. The Lord Jesus said that the tree that bore no fruit would be cut off. It seems harsh, but if we really convince him that we want it, he enables us to come to maturity.

There needed to be a balance in the face of this Lion that this painter knew nothing about. Then I realized that many people fell into one of these two mistakes: one where they see God as a merciless being, out to get them for any and every mistake they made, or a dumb God where they could basically get away with murder as long as they had said the sinner's prayer or been baptized (or whatever their tradition dictated) at some point in their life.

To the best of my ability, I told the painter that though Aslan was forgiving, he was also stern. The third time around, he nailed it. Now *this* was the Lion that C.S. Lewis had

had so much inspiration and clarity in writing about!

I could have never predicted how much Lisa would love this painting.

At the end of the night, we all sat down after a hearty meal to read through a few chapters here and there of the seven books of *The Chronicles of Narnia.* One of the chapters I chose to read through was the last one of *The Silver Chair,* when Jill and Eustace find the lost prince. The king of Narnia is old and on his deathbed when his lost heir is finally found. The king sees his son, for whom he has been searching, for only a brief minute after the son was rescued from ten years of captivity, and then the king dies. The trumpets sound and the nation of Narnia mourns the death of their sovereign. But it is not completely hopeless, because they have found his successor.

Stephen and I had both been so moved when I read it out loud to him for the first time. It made me think of all the men and women who have gone before us with the firm conviction that something special was

going to happen in their lifetime, that the Lord would come back, that a new wave of a great awakening would return like it did years before. But they have passed on, and none of that happened. I had always wondered why that was.

My grandfather had longed for that day to come in his lifetime. Clayt Sonmore, George Warnock, and so many others had too. It would seem as if they never witnessed what they had truly wanted and had preached about. But then I realized that they had seen hope. When they saw us, the new generation of lost princes, come to life again after years of being slaves of this dark underground world, they saw the salvation of the Lord, just like Simeon did when he saw the Lord Jesus Christ as a baby in Israel: "Then he took him up in his arms and blessed God and said, Lord, now let thy slave depart in peace, according to thy word, for mine eyes have seen thy saving health" (Luke 2:28–30).

The Narnia Party

All that is gold does not glitter,
Not all those who wander are lost;
The old that is strong does not wither,
Deep roots are not reached by the frost.

From the ashes a fire shall be woken,
A light from the shadows shall spring;
Renewed shall be blade that was broken,
The crown-less again shall be king.
J.R.R. Tolkien[18]

---

18 The Lord Of the Rings Trilogy written by J.R.R Tolkien
published by George Allen & Unwin

Afterword
Let Us Return to the Roots of Our Godly Heritage

(An edited version of an address given by Russell Martín Stendal in Cottonwood, Arizona, October 2018, at a conference celebrating the tenth anniversary of SOM)

WILLIAM TYNDALE'S New Testament, published in 1534, was called the "Plowboy" Edition. In a day and age when many claimed that the Scriptures were only for the clergy and that someone had to be educated in order to be able to handle the Bible, Tyndale's reply to one such learned man was: "If God spare my life, ere many years I will cause a boy that driveth the plow to know more of the Scripture than thou dost."

This paved the way for the heritage we have in the English-speaking world due to the written Scriptures. The Great Awakening happened to English-speaking people. The Spanish-speaking world has never known an awakening like that, but maybe it will. For the first fifteen hundred years of Christianity, most people didn't have the possibility of having their own copy of the Scriptures. And even if they could have afforded the manuscripts, the vast majority of the people didn't know how to read. The first schools that became the public schools came out of the Great Awakening. We still, in many of our churches, have what we call Sunday school. But the first Sunday school was all day long because it was the only day that the workers had off, and it was to teach them to read the Bible because the average person didn't know how to read; they didn't have school

materials, so the textbook was the King James Bible.

Now, people take healthcare for granted, but Christians started the first medical care or hospitals, like the Sunday schools, as an outreach to everyone. And it transformed England and spread to the United States. Three waves of the Great Awakening hit the United States, and this could have continued, except that modernism set in. Modernism began to redefine key words of the Scriptures. At first it just seemed as if educated people were trying to put their spin on the ball, but soon it became apparent that what they were doing was denying the possibility of victorious Christian living. And that has taken root and put out the fire in our churches and particularly affected our young people.

If you look across modern America and go to an average Sunday morning service and observe the Sunday schools that are still in operation, you will be acutely aware of the fact that there is a shortage particularly of the males between the ages of fourteen and forty in church today (and a shortage of young people in general). Unless that reverses, Christianity in North America is going to go the same route as it did in Western Europe where it is at extremely low ebb. I've seen it change in my lifetime here in the US. We are due for another spiritual awakening, and if it doesn't happen, in fifteen or twenty years, devastation will have completely set in.

If the new generations don't catch fire for God here in North America, the possibility of turning our society around will be lost – who knows for how long. Now if we look at it from a global perspective, God is moving tremendously in places where it doesn't seem like he used to move. The Muslim world hasn't seen much in the line of conversion to Christianity for most of its history. It has only been in the last five or ten years that the trend has reversed, and we have seen a significant amount of Muslims converted; this is going up on a geometric progression. The Spanish-speaking world is being lit on fire for God like never before.

Our family went to Colombia in 1964 when less than one half of one percent of the

population was evangelical Christian, and the country had just come out of a time of great persecution in which many evangelical Christians had been killed – between 1948 and 1958 – in what was known as The Great Violence. Today it is estimated that Colombia is 25% evangelical Christian, and this is surging. Now, unfortunately, among that 25% of the population that is now classed as evangelical Christian, we can't guarantee that all these people are actually born again and being led by the Spirit of God. If we could measure that – which we can't because we can't judge people's hearts – the number would be much lower, but still extremely significant and going up, not down.

Most don't realize to what extent our English language has been influenced by our heritage in the Bible. Cultures in other parts of the world don't have a heritage of almost five hundred years in the Bible like we do. William Tyndale's plowboy edition of the Scriptures was published in 1534. It won't be long until we hit the 500th anniversary. William Tyndale had to smuggle the Bibles into England, and the Bishop continued to oppose him. The sly bishop decided to buy up the Bibles, buy up the New Testaments and burn them, and get rid of the threat. But William Tyndale outsmarted him because for every New Testament that the bishop bought and burned, Tyndale used the money to print three or four more.

Unfortunately, William Tyndale's translation of the second half of the Old Testament was lost in a shipwreck at sea. It seems that the only book that survived, curiously, was the book of Jonah. Other people, starting with Matthew Henry, had to retranslate the latter half of the Old Testament because Tyndale was killed before he could redo the work that was lost. So the last half of the Old Testament in many translations, including the King James, doesn't have the same terminology and isn't translated the same way as the first half of the Old Testament. That turned out to be a little bit unfortunate.

It does not involve big changes, but there is a difference between synonyms. Many

different synonyms are used to translate a given Hebrew word over the course of most English translations of the Bible. And because the latter half of the Old Testament is called the prophetic part, and that is the part most quoted by Jesus and the apostles in the New Testament, it has made it so that some of the prophetic Scriptures in English have been a bit blurred, because the same thing is not translated the same way, and you can't compare apples to apples and oranges to oranges.

So when I did the Jubilee Bible translation into Spanish, I discovered that one man, who was the last scholar to have learned Hebrew as a living language (with the Jews as the Inquisition was expelling them from Spain), did a very consistent translation. Before leaving the Catholic Church, he was a monk, and there was a Hebrew Bible chained to a post in his monastery; they worshipped it and kissed it, but nobody knew how to read it. That is, until he started taking in and protecting Jews who were being persecuted and killed by the Inquisition. He had an underground railroad to get those Jews out of Spain and into other countries.

This monk learned Hebrew and began to translate the Hebrew Bible into Spanish. Of course the Inquisition went after him with everything that they had. It's a long story, but out of 3,000 Bibles that were eventually published in 1569, the Inquisition destroyed most of them. Very few copies survived, and today, a few are in museums or in the hands of collectors.

There hasn't been significant Bible distribution into Spanish-speaking countries prior to World War II. So these countries don't have a heritage in the Scriptures. But another interesting fact is that Spanish speakers love to read, and having a Bible is a prestige item (plus many countries where we work such as Colombia, Cuba, and Venezuela have very high literacy). So when we give people Bibles, they read them. If you give away a Bible in Colombia, even if the person you give it to isn't going to read it, someone will read it. If we give it to a soldier on the battlefield who doesn't want to carry it and

read it, he'll send it home and his mother will read it, or his wife or fiancée will read it. Or he'll simply horse trade it to another soldier who wants it and who will read it.

The Bibles that we place and give away get read until they fall apart, because few know the history, the people are curious, and the Holy Spirit begins to draw them.

Have you ever thought of the funny sayings that we have in English? There are things that unless you knew where they came from in the Bible, they just wouldn't make sense. Have you ever heard of someone being saved with "the skin of their teeth?" Do you know where that comes from? It is from the book of Job. Do you know why it's there? How would you ever come up with "the skin of your teeth?" What in the world is this? And yet we rattle that off every now and then without thinking.

The word "skin" in Hebrew[19] has to do with the covering of our natural body. Adam

---

19 Remember that Biblical Hebrew only has about 5,000 key words, and now an English dictionary can have up to 500,000 words.

and Eve found out early on that without the covering of God, they were naked. If we're left alone in our natural covering which is our bare skin, we're the only species of animal that would be considered naked. So there is obviously something different about us from the rest of the creation. We are designed in such a way that we have to be covered, and spiritually our covering has to do with the Spirit of God.

There are all kinds of man-made coverings. What did Adam and Eve do when they realized they were naked? They sewed fig leaves together. Someone said that was the first attempt at religion. They were trying to cover things up, but they couldn't get the root of the problem dealt with. Do you remember how God solved that situation, even though he had to expel them from the garden? God provided them with leather girdles. How do you get a leather girdle? How do you get leather? Something has to die. This has to do with blood sacrifice. So the only way that we can be covered and protected and brought back into fellowship with God is to come

under the covering of the Holy Spirit, who has been provided because Jesus came and died for us as the Lamb of God that takes away the sin of the world.

Getting back to the ancient book of Job (where key terminology was being set and things were being developed, such that sometimes you couldn't tell until a millennium or so later), what in the world was Job talking about when he said he was *saved with the skin of his teeth?*

Now teeth symbolize a lot of things. In the animal world, teeth aren't there just for eating; they can also be used for offense or defense. That's what that word teeth there implies. The book of Job sets out a fundamental difference between God and Satan. It's the first book in the Bible where Satan is named. Out of fifty-five references of Satan in the Bible, fifteen are in the book of Job. And Satan is not only named, but he is also revealed for who he is and what he does.

That is why the philosophy of Job's friends didn't hold true because they didn't know about Satan, and they didn't realize what Satan is really doing. If you want to understand what is going on in the world today, if you want to understand what is going on in Washington D.C. right now even in the last couple of weeks, if you don't understand who Satan is and what he is about and what he is doing, you will not be able to understand or make sense out of the news.

God held up Job as a sterling example and in effect Satan said, "Yeah, but that is because you protect him, and you bless him. Take that away and he will curse you to your face." When God authorized Satan, and God removed his protection from around Job, Satan chewed into Job with all his might. He wasn't really authorized to kill Job's children, but he did. He wasn't really authorized to kill all Job's servants, and he did – except for four servants who came back with the news. Satan never knows when to quit. He always overplays his hand. Look at it this way: Job *escaped with the skin of his teeth* (Job 19:20).

In other words his teeth, his ability to chew into someone else to protect himself, had a covering. His covering was his fear of

God – his fear of the Lord. Satan had no skin on his teeth. No covering. He was willing to take brute force and use it to the max, with absolutely no inhibitions. And Satan still doesn't understand; he's never understood the ways of God. God doesn't define himself by his use of brute force. God lets people produce whatever kind of fruit they are going to produce. He gives every one of us opportunity, after opportunity, after opportunity. He doesn't destroy us the first time we make a little mistake. He lets our life be defined by either one of two ways: We are either going to go our own way, and we're going to fall into the devil's trap. Or else, we'll seek God and surrender to God and go God's way. That's the only way to produce the lasting fruit of righteousness.

Those who go God's way – those who belong to God – no matter what happens, no matter what they lose, no matter how bad the enemy attacks are, they never use enemy tactics. God's people always have skin on their teeth. If we belong to God, if he has truly changed and transformed our hearts, then we treat others the way we would be desire to be treated. Then for us the fear of the Lord is the beginning of wisdom. And we don't do things because it's convenient. We don't do things just because we can, or we have the power or the ability to dominate someone or even to destroy them. No! We operate in the fear of the Lord. And all of our desires for revenge or for vengeance, we leave all of that with God.

We don't put footnotes in the Jubilee Bible to put our own theological spin. The purpose of the footnotes is if we are unable to do a direct or literal translation. One of the few places where we hit this was with the Hebrew word for "redeemer." Do you remember in the Jewish tradition, the eldest son got a double portion of the inheritance? They would come into their inheritance at age thirty. One of the reasons that the eldest son got the double portion was because the oldest male in the family is responsible for everyone else.

If someone in the family got into trouble, if someone was taken hostage or someone got into such a terrible predicament that they had to sell themselves or even their family

and their lands into servitude, the kinsman-redeemer had the moral and the spiritual obligation to ransom and to redeem. That is why they were given a double portion. They had that responsibility.

But that word "redeemer," (the exact same word) is also translated "avenger" of blood. The kinsman-redeemer and the avenger of blood is the same person; it's the same word. So in order for us to bring that out in English, we have to footnote the Bible that when it says "avenger" of blood, it is the exact same word as redeemer. If we want to know how many times the word redeemer is used in Scripture, we have to also count the times that it says avenger.

Spiritually, since we are incapable of redeeming ourselves and we are not capable of redeeming anyone else, God also wants us to lay down any desires that we have to be the avenger. This is because Jesus is our kinsman-Redeemer, and he is also the Avenger of blood, and we leave it in his hands. And he does some very, very interesting things. When Jesus was describing what was going to happen in the judgment day, he said he was going to separate the sheep from the goats. The sheep are those that have a different nature inside than the goats. Goats don't care what they feed on. Goats don't care if the water is clean or if it is dirty. The sheep do.

Jesus said that the goats were going to be separated to his left and the sheep were going to go to his right. The sheep were going to enter into the kingdom, and the goats were going to go to eternal perdition. His criterion for dividing these two was very, very interesting. He said, "When I was hungry, you fed me. When I was thirsty you gave me to drink. When I was sick you visited me. When I was in prison, you visited me." And the redeemed said, "But Lord, we don't remember doing anything like that to you." And he said, "When you did it to the least of any of my brethren, you did it to me."

Then to the ones who are lost he said, "When you didn't do it to me, when you didn't have concern or care to even the least of my brethren" (Matthew 25:35–37, 40, 45, paraphrased).

Can you imagine that? Can you imagine the trouble they got into just because they had the opportunity where they could have cared for someone who belonged to God but they didn't do it? Now what's going to happen to those who actually went out with evil intent and harmed someone belonging to the family of God?

Let me backtrack and say that Jesus, according to Colossians 1:16–20, according to John 1:1, and according to many Scriptures was there with the Father from the very beginning and was involved in the creation of all things. Jesus participated in everything. There is nothing that was made without him being involved, of things that are seen and things that are unseen. So as our Creator, he has a right and an authority over every living thing, and now doubly so as our Redeemer who gave his life as a ransom for us. That gives him double authority.

To those who have attacked his family and done something bad to any of those who are his, even to the most insignificant member of the family, he is also the Avenger of blood. This gives him a triple right to declare judgment and to see that it is carried out. Jesus, however, doesn't think the way the devil does. You see, the devil doesn't understand anything about the ways of God. He is totally ignorant to the way of the cross. Satan couldn't even imagine that Jesus would be willing to give his life for us. He couldn't imagine that the Father would be willing to give his only Son. The devil thought that if he could manage to kill Jesus he would win. And when Jesus died, God won and opened the way for all of us into his victory.

Jesus loves to redeem. Redemption is in his very nature. He loves to extend a way out to those that are hopelessly lost. And so, when you have those who were killing Christians and persecuting the church like the apostle Paul when he was known as Saul of Tarsus, Jesus could have totally destroyed him on the road to Damascus. That would have been righteous and just, and Saul of Tarsus would have thoroughly deserved it. But guess what Jesus decided to do with him? He didn't even ask him the question. None of our formulas

for evangelism fit with Saul of Tarsus. Nobody explained the four points, or the seven points. He didn't come forward in an altar call. Nobody had him repeat a sinner's prayer. None of that happened.

Jesus revealed himself from heaven, and the glory of God was so strong that it blinded Saul and dropped him flat on his face. Then Jesus told him, *Arise and go into the city, and it shall be told thee what it behooves thee to do* (Acts 9:6). Then the Lord spoke to a disciple named Ananias (who was at first reluctant to have anything to do with the fearsome Saul of Tarsus) telling him, *For I will show him [Saul] how much it behooves him to suffer for my name* (Acts 9:16). Jesus gave Saul of Tarsus the opportunity to replace people that he had helped martyr, such as Stephen and others.

These are secrets of the kingdom of God that we have also seen developed in the mission field. For many years, Colombia was known as the country where more pastors and more missionaries, and where more Christians were being killed than any other place on the planet. Just one rebel leader is thought to have had more than four hundred pastors killed. We've worked with many widows of pastors that were martyred. But guess what? After the missionaries fled, after the pastors fled, after the pastors that didn't flee were killed, guess what God started doing? He started reaching the rebels. He started going after the people that were causing the trouble. He started taking these men and women and turning them around.

Some of the first ones to turn to the Lord in the Marxist guerrilla camps and in the communist guerrilla movement in general were ruthlessly wiped out. We were dealing with something that had as strong as a spirit as what is presently going on in North Korea, a spirit that wants to wipe out all mention of God.

There are evil spirits that will start out by trying to twist the terminology of the Scriptures, trying to take the edge off the sword of the Christian, trying to tell us that God's goal for us isn't really victory, and that victory is impossible. They tell the church,

"We have to sin in word, thought, deed, and by omission every day."

Have you ever been told that? They say, "It's our human condition. We can't avoid it." And with that last one, they've really got you because even if you manage to make it through the day without any bad thoughts and without any bad words or deeds, how in the world can you make it past the last one because there are so many great things you could have done and you didn't do, so you've sinned by omission. So they have you conditioned to live in a defeated state.

Well the truth is that all of us are hopeless sinners, but Jesus Christ is not. And he wants to live inside of every one of us and reign and rule from our hearts. So there is at least one part of us that can be totally transformed and redeemed now even in our human condition, and that is our heart! He can come in and change and transform our heart and change our basic motivation. And yes, we still have human limitations, but the Scriptures say: *For a just man falls seven times and rises up again, but the wicked shall fall into evil* (Proverbs 24:16).

You see friends, if we fall, it depends a lot on what direction we were pointed at when we went down. If we have Jesus in our heart, our heart is going to be to serve God. And yes, the Enemy may lay some ambushes for us and yes, there may be some things that need to be refined in our life, but the basic desire of our heart will be to serve God as long as Jesus is on the throne of our life. That will never change. And if we need discipline, if we need correction, God the Father will provide it if we are truly his children. That is the wonderful thing about serving God.

In our ministry, we haven't got time to run a detective agency to see what everybody is doing. And if someone gets out of line to the point where the board or the ministry has to intervene, that is a pretty late solution. Chances are, a lot of serious damage has already taken place. But you see if we want to be disciplined by God the Father, he'll catch it early. He likes to deal with things when they are starting to go wrong – when it is just a wrong desire in our heart, before there have been any nasty words or any evil deeds.

Sometimes we wonder why we go through trials and tribulations. And Jesus said every true believer would go through trials and tribulations. Everyone's faith will be tried. You don't have to live in a country like Colombia where so many pastors have been killed. No. You can be right here in comfortable North America, and if you decide to go all out for God, your faith will be tried one way or another.

But God will be there and will prove himself greater than any trial and any tribulation that there ever possibly could be. And he will never allow us to be in a situation where there is no way out because he is the way. As he brings us forth in victory, and as we overcome whatever it is that the devil has laid in our path trying to trip us up, when we win those victories, we don't just win a personal victory or a victory for our family. When God brings us forth in victory, we win the ability to be an example for others. We win the ability to minister grace and truth to others that are coming along behind. You see how that works?

It isn't just an intellectual process of sharing principles and values. No, when we've been on the frontlines of the battle, and when God has seen us through, he gives us the ability so that there can actually be an impartation to our children, to our grandchildren, to those who God places us in contact with in ministry. Early on in the Scripture, starting with the Ten Commandments, it says that the sins of the fathers affect until the third and the fourth generation of those that hate God but that he will show mercy on those that love God and keep his commandments unto thousands of generations (Exodus 20:5–6). Literally translated, the word "thousand" in Hebrew has to do with perfection. It means that when we obey God, a dynamic goes into place in generation after generation, and things get better and better. In my family, I am the third generation in the ministry. My children are the fourth generation in ministry. And now I have grandchildren that want to be in ministry.

Among the Páez Indigenous people that we're working with, God started working with them and sent Canadian missionaries in 1932. Recently, we brought some Canadian ladies on a missions trip who brought huge duffle bags full of yarn, among other things, because they were going to teach the Páez people how to knit. Well, somehow they got all this through customs and got out there and we brought a number of Indigenous ladies out from the mountains in one of their typical, colorful busses. They knitted all that yarn up in nothing flat. The only reason why they hadn't done this before is because they couldn't find that material locally. And the Canadians were really impressed with the stitches. They wondered how had they come up with that? And the wife of one of the pastors said, "Oh real easy, Canadian missionaries came in 1932 and taught those stitches to my grandparents."

When things go well, God multiplies. God puts things up in a geometric progression. But the sins of the fathers can affect to the third and to the fourth generation. Have you noticed what's going on in America? Who are the ones that are getting the abortions? Is it the God-fearing Christian people that are out there getting the abortions? No. It is those who are not being moved by the fear of God. Those are the ones who are getting the abortions, and it is not only affecting their future, it is cutting off the future generations. And those people that are doing that are living in a lifestyle that is not approved by God.

Now if somebody gets an abortion or if somebody is living a lesbian or a homosexual lifestyle, we can still befriend them and be available so that the grace of God can reach them. It isn't our job to condemn them, even though we don't agree with their lifestyle. But if we tell them the truth, we can truthfully tell them that what they are doing is sterile. They are never going to have any heirs. They won't have any children; they won't have any grandchildren. There will be no one to look after them in their old age. When they become a liability, their friends may turn their backs on them. And if Christian people don't

reach out to them, they will not ever have any real friends. That's the truth of the matter.

We need to think and meditate about this: *For God so loved the world, that he gave his only begotten Son* … doesn't mean that God has warm, fuzzy, feelings for the world. It doesn't mean that he is emotionally attached to the world. It doesn't mean that he approves of the world. There are two words for love in Greek, and the word that is used there is the word *agapao;* we don't have an equivalent in English. Our words for mercy and for charity don't have a verb form. But when it says, *God so loved the world,* it means he chose to have charity, to have mercy on the world and not just leave those that are in the world to go and continue into total destruction.

God decided to put a stop to the evil that Satan planted by sending his own Son, Jesus. I believe that God wants to turn the course of history. The devil has told us and he has told the church that we can't win. And don't get me wrong; I don't believe that we are to necessarily take over the kingdoms of this world, but if God does place someone in a position of authority such as Daniel, they are responsible, and that responsibility can be well used. There is much that can be done today to further the cause of liberty by yielding to the direction and guidance of the Holy Spirit (Genesis 45:7; 2 Corinthians 3:17).

Colombia, as a nation, is addicted to the drug traffic. The peace treaty that we were involved in, for the most part, stopped the killing of Christians, stopped the killing of pastors, and stopped the burning of church buildings, but it didn't stop the drug traffic. And that is where a moral battle rages now that also affects North America and Europe (where most of the drugs are being consumed).

Venezuela is experiencing a national breakdown due to rampant corruption and many other factors. Inflation just hit one million percent. Yet the opportunity for the gospel is unprecedented. As a result of all the unrest in Colombia and Venezuela, there are millions of displaced persons. This is, of course, a terrible tragedy, but it is also a tremendous opportunity for ministry to those

who have lost the things of this world. And there continue to be many similar situations all around the globe. Now is the time for the people of God to make the very best use of our time and resources as we wait for the imminent return of our Lord Jesus Christ.

Connect with the Stendal's Ministry

For more information on the Stendals Ministry, and to find out the latest news on how to pray for Colombia visit the following websites:

Website
www.cpcsociety.ca
www.spiritofmartyrdom.com/

Receive newsletter updates
spiritofmartyrdom.com/application-form/
(Check the Latin America box to get the latest newsletter on the Stendal's Ministry)

Buy books
http://amzn.to/1nPLcNL